THE PREROGATIVE OF GOD MY JOURNEY WITH LEUKEMIA

A STORY OF RESTORATION AND HEALING

ARLINE FARQUHARSON

PRESS

Blessings!

A.P. Farquharson

Acknowledgments

I would like to thank my family members for supporting me and taking care of me during my time of illness. Special thanks to those who went beyond the call, investing time and money and many hours to drive me around or just to make my home livable for my return from the hospital. It has not gone unnoticed.

Thanks to the pastors and members of the Palm Bay Seventh-Day Adventist Church, who constantly kept me before the throne of grace and prayed unceasingly for my recovery.

Thanks to Miss Phoebe and her family and the prison ministry team for their unshakable faith that God would come through for me.

I also want to thank the individuals who took the time to text me every morning and night just to see how my day or night went. I want you to know how much I appreciate you for being in my corner and for building me up when I got totally discouraged. I am ever so grateful for the counsels that I received that helped to keep my eyes open for impending crises.

Sincere thanks also to those who tried so hard to keep me healthy with different remedies and for their outpouring of love and thanks to those of you who offered words of inspiration and encouragement, always knowing just the right words to say. Thank you all, it meant a lot in my time of need.

Most of all, I want to thank God for His faithfulness, His mercy and grace through whom I'm able to do this. I write this testimony because of a test that I believe God allowed. May His name forever be glorified.

CONTENTS

PREFACE

*T*his book is written to share and hopefully encourage anyone on his or her own journey and to give a reference point from which I try to tell my story. This was a journey I would rather not have taken. The book is a compilation of stories and events as they occurred during my journey with AML Leukemia. It gives insights into how God works for His people even when we can't see how or even when we don't expect it.

This is the story of a spiritual journey that took me through what I refer to as "the valley of the shadow of death." It goes through many twists and turns and sometimes was more of a roller coaster ride than anything else. I was diagnosed, received treatment and went to remission. Then I had a relapse, received treatment, and went to remission again for a second time. I subsequently had a stem cell transplant and even as I write, I am completely dependent on God as to how this will all turn out. It's all in His hands.

I want to tell my story so others may be strengthened by one person's experiences. If you are going through difficult circumstances, I want you to know that there is power in prayer and that God is in control of all our life situations. I just want to remind you that there can be no testimony about our faith and the goodness of God, or His mercy and His grace, unless we have experienced it ourselves — "our test."

Writing this book has been a challenge for me, but my desire is that others with cancer or those close to them will find some help from reading its pages.

My hope is that if you are going through a similar experience you will find encouragement and insights here that will help you through the tough times and that you will know that there is hope in Jesus. There is indeed a light at the end of the tunnel and you can make the journey with Christ who promises never to leave you nor forsake you.

THE PREROGATIVE OF GOD

Romans 11:33: "O the depth of the riches both of the wisdom and knowledge of God! How unsearchable are His judgments and His ways past finding out."

*W*ho can explain the way God thinks?

In January of 2012, I was working on the second year of my tenure as director of the outreach ministry for my church. I felt that I needed some help with programming for the new year, since I did not have an assistant the year prior. I thought it would be easier to coordinate more outreach programs, so I asked Earl. He agreed and I submitted his name to the church board, where he was elected as my assistant in February 2012.

Earl had worked in the outreach ministry for the previous year and was instrumental in providing outreach materials for the department. He was enthusiastic and

11

willing to do whatever was asked of him. I was, therefore, confident that he could make a difference for the new year. At this time, neither of us knew what was ahead of us. We launched a few programs, which he spearheaded, and I felt comfortable that this could work.

Halfway through the year, I started feeling tired from exertion; I tried to ignore it or blame it on lack of sleep, or anything else that would fit. Then on August 8, 2012, I was diagnosed with AML leukemia, and Earl had to take control of the department. After my diagnosis, I was sent for treatment to a cancer center in the Tampa area. Then on January 1, 2013, after returning home, I was told that Earl was diagnosed with leukemia (CLL). I was astounded. How is this possible? How coincidental was it that two people from the same department would both have leukemia?

I went to see Earl immediately and found that indeed there was something wrong. He had begun to lose weight and was not the individual he was when I left Palm Bay for my treatment. We struggled to understand this phenomenon and even joked about it somewhat. I visited with Earl on occasion, and we would compare notes as to the differences in our symptoms.

He liked coconut water and I mentioned to his wife that I could get him a gallon each week if she would like. She accepted the offer and would call me on Saturday nights to say yes or no for the next week.

I would pick up the coconut water and then be reimbursed when I delivered it. I was able to purchase the fresh coconut water from a gentleman who brought coconuts from somewhere around the West Palm/Hollywood area. He would cut them open while I waited, then pour them in gallon jugs, which were for Earl and me. It was just something I thought I could do to brighten his day.

He started to receive chemotherapy, and I later found out that his oncologist and my hematologist shared the same office. While visiting with him one Sabbath, he mentioned he was going for chemo at the doctor's office on Monday; I mentioned my appointment was on Tuesday. I forgot about the conversation until I took my car in for service early Monday morning. When the service was completed, I got in my car to go back home and it was then that I heard the voice telling me to go to my doctor's office. I was not obedient — I simply said there was no point going there today when I have to be there tomorrow. I turned the car in the direction of the interstate to make my way home, but the voice kept telling me that I should go to the doctor's office. I did not have peace in my decision to go home, so I finally turned the car around, just before getting on the highway, and made my way to the doctor's office.

When I got there, I saw Earl standing at the reception desk signing in for his appointment. When he saw me, he smiled and asked what I was doing there; I remarked that this was my doctor's office too. He asked me if I had an appointment and I told him no, so he quickly asked, "so what are you doing here?" I said the first thing that came to my mind: "I came to sit with you."

I had struggled with my decision to do what God was telling me to do, but God's will prevailed, and we were both pleased at the outcome.

There were times during his IV chemotherapy treatment when I felt so gratified that I was sent there to help whether it was to give a glass of water, a blanket, or just a mint or cough drops. I was there to do anything I could to make him comfortable as we passed the time waiting for his chemotherapy treatment to end.

I got a deep sense that God, who had put this plan in motion, was there with us. When the treatment was over, we got in the car to go home so he called the person scheduled to pick him up and told them not to come because he had a ride, unexpected but orchestrated by God.

On the way home, I thought of a natural food café, why that came into my mind I will never know. The inner voice spoke to me and said, "you should take him there." I thought, *I already passed the turn to go there.* The voice said, "you should take him there."

Why do I always resist? Without thinking, the words came out of my mouth. "I know a natural food café where we could get some fresh carrot juice."

He was so excited I could not tell him I already passed the turn to get to it. I simply said, "If you want to go I'll take you."

He said, "Sure, thank you," and again I turned the car around.

When we got to the café, I left him in the car and went in to get us both a glass of fresh raw organic carrot juice, which we thoroughly enjoyed. I took him home on Monday evening, his wife told me he did well on Tuesday after the chemotherapy, but late Wednesday night, she had to take him to the emergency room. I visited with her in the hospital on Thursday while we waited for the outcome of his visit. As the day wore on and more family members began to arrive, I left the hospital to go home. Later that evening, I received a call telling me that Earl had passed away.

I struggled with that for quite a while. I just couldn't understand why God would take him and leave me. I had been sick much longer than him. It was such a short time since his diagnosis. There had to be a good reason which was beyond my comprehension. Then I was reminded of the verse in Isaiah 55:8-9: "'For my thoughts are not your thoughts, neither are your ways my ways,' saith the Lord. 'For as the heavens are higher than the earth, so are my ways higher than your ways, and my thoughts than your thoughts.'"

We can't explain in human terms what God chooses to do in the lives of His children. All we can do is trust that He knows what is best. I kept thinking how terrible I would have felt if I didn't finally obey God's voice! I thanked Him for giving me the opportunity to do something for Him even through the protests. I am so grateful that God is longsuffering and does not treat any of us as we deserve.

God rewarded me that day, by allowing me to have my appointment while I was there in the office so I did not have to make the trip the next day. This was all initiated by my doctor without my asking. She calmly said, "Why don't I see you now since you are already here and your report is back?"

I was also given a sizable concession on my bill that I did not expect and probably would not have gotten if I had not been there at that precise time. I walked out of the office praising God and rejoicing at what had just taken place. Despite my disobedience, God was so incredibly faithful.

THE DIAGNOSIS

*I*t was early on Sunday morning, August 8, 2012, that I went into my backyard to plant some calaloo (spinach-like) seedlings given to me by one of the ladies from my church. Knowing I wanted to start a vegetable garden, she was generous. I went out early before the sun came up because in Florida, it gets pretty warm by 8:00 a.m in early August. The days get hot as soon as the sun hits the horizon.

I started on my mission because I didn't want the plants to die. I had them in water from Friday and over the Sabbath. I was afraid they would not last much longer if I didn't plant them right away. I started planting the first six seedlings and felt a bit light headed and short of breath, so I quickly made my way to my family room where I was able to make it to my big recliner. I decided to sit for a while to cool off. *The sun is a bit too much for me*, I thought. As I was feeling a bit warm from my experience, I asked my granddaughter to turn on the ceiling fan. Before long, the feelings subsided and I started to feel better. That should have been a warning that something was wrong, but I ignored it and as soon as I felt a little better, I went right back outside and continued my project to get those plants in the ground. Soon the lightheadedness came back, but this time worse than it did before, so I started planting two seedlings in one hole just to make sure I planted them all. By that point, I felt like I was going to pass out, so I made my way back into the house and stayed there until my son got home.

God had it all planned out. My son lives in Virginia and just happened to be at my house for a visit with his two children. He left the children at home with me while he went to the airport to pick up his wife. She was not able to travel down to Florida with them by car at the time they left Virginia, but she flew down later to join them. I believe God orchestrated the whole thing so I would have help at the time I needed it.

When I had to hear that horrific diagnosis, I had family with me. I believe that was all God and was no coincidence. I was able to say to my son, "You need to take me to the emergency room."

He had just left me a few hours earlier and I seemed fine, so the request was quite a surprise for him. Understandably he asked, "Now?"

I made my way to the emergency room. After a number of blood tests, one nurse remarked that she had only seen values like those in people who have had chemotherapy. She assumed she had a contaminated sample so she drew the sample again and walked it to the lab herself. She returned with the same results. The doctors agreed to admit me to the local hospital because as they put it, my hemoglobin of 4.0 was too low for them to send me home. (The hemoglobin carries the oxygen in the blood around the body.) As one nurse remarked, I should not have been able to walk around with a value that low.

Now, I had an explanation for my tiredness, shortness of breath, and lightheadedness. Thinking the concern was only my low hemoglobin, I figured that it would be no problem and an easy fix — a few iron shots and I will be as good as new, or so I thought. As a matter of fact, I had already started taking prenatal vitamins a week or two earlier because I felt my iron had to be low since I was so tired. I had diagnosed myself as being anemic, so taking the vitamins should have taken care of it. This was not a surprise for me; being anemic was actually a condition I was used to. I expected to go home in a few days with a prescription for iron pills after they took care of this little problem and I would be just fine. The result was more than I bargained for.

Before I knew what was taking place, unbeknownst to me, my primary care physician and a hematologist were called to see me in the hospital. The next morning, they both showed up in my hospital room. I was pleased to see my doctor, since it had been a while since I had last seen him. I was also extremely happy to see a face I knew.

He introduced me to the hematologist. I was optimistic that all would be well, so I did not expect to hear bad news. Then they broke the news to me that I had Acute Myeloid Leukemia. The presentation was so smooth; it was as though they rehearsed their part before entering the room. I suspected that in order to cushion the blow, they quickly explained that they would get me the best care so I did not need to worry.

They decided to send me to a cancer center in Tampa and my journey began.

Can you imagine what it was like to hear the words "you have leukemia"? I went to the emergency room, fully expected to come back home with a prescription for a medication that would take care of whatever the problem was, but I never expected to be away from home for an extended period of time. I had no real information on leukemia, except what I heard about others who have had it, and none of it was good. I did not understand the real ramification of having the disease; I had no idea how much trouble I was in and did not try to find out. I thought that the less I knew about it, the less I had to worry about it. To be honest, at first I really didn't take it seriously, that is, until the hematologist came in the room and told me that if I didn't get immediate aggressive treatment, I could die within three weeks.

To prove her point, the hematologist decided I needed a bone marrow biopsy quickly and she would do it herself if it came down to it. One day, while she was doing her rounds, she was anxious to know if the biopsy was done. Because we had waited a while to have it done, she wanted to be sure the diagnosis was indeed

Acute Myeloid Leukemia (AML). She decided to do it herself, before leaving the hospital for the day.

After the biopsy, she was sure that I needed to be at the cancer center right away. Both doctors had agreed on where they wanted me to go, and they were confident that it was the place where I would get the best treatment, and have the best opportunity for recovery/remission.

My doctor (I call her "Dr. Lisa") is a praying woman, who had God at the center of her life and her practice. It was evident in the way she treated her patients. We could always depend on her for a word of prayer before leaving her office. She felt that she was a conduit through which God could perform His miracles for her patients. As she prayed with me, I felt a peace about her handling my disease and recovery. She was so positive that I wanted to believe because she did.

I remained in the Palm Bay Hospital for eight days after the diagnosis, waiting for a bed in the cancer center. I requested to go home, but my doctor said I needed to go from "bed to bed." I had no idea what he meant until weeks later when I got a good grasp of my situation. When I called him in desperation, he never told me anything had changed about my situation, but I felt better about everything. Dr. Prieto never acted as if I was making unreasonable requests and he never appeared weary of having to explain to me what was happening and what we needed to do. He took the time and I am so thankful for him. I call him my faithful friend.

I went to the cancer center by ambulance at night. We left the hospital around 8:00 p.m. Here I was, driving across Florida, not knowing where I was going or what to expect. I can't begin to imagine what I would have done had I known what was ahead of me. I arrived at the hospital about around 11:00 p.m. on the night of August 16, 2012, where I remained until my discharge sixty-five days later.

After admission to the cancer center, I decided that I would continue to call on God for help but decided I would not yet tell anyone at church. It was a devastating blow to me and I felt that my witness was destroyed. The pride in me kicked in and I began to imagine all the things that would be said. After all, I was the person who was an advocate for a good diet and nutrition and now, I had cancer. It did not take long, however, before the majority of the church knew about my diagnosis and

TRYING TO
MAKE SENSE OF IT ALL

My first response to the diagnosis was denial — I didn't believe it. I said, "that diagnosis cannot be mine; it must be a mistake," because I had been eating a raw diet for over three years prior to this discovery. I wasn't sick for those years and thought I was doing well, and then suddenly here I was. Could it be that the minute I slacked off from my routine and started eating cooked foods that I would get sick? I was really dumbfounded and confused. What went wrong? How could this be?

My story began back in 2008, after my mother died. I moved to Florida from Rochester, New York because my mother, who lived and taught in Jamaica, West Indies, could not tolerate the cold in upstate New York: what I called, "the freezer next door to Canada." My mother came to visit every year during her summers off from school. My siblings and I were concerned about her traveling back and forth so often as she was getting older. She worked well past age seventy before retiring. It had gotten so bad that someone had to fly down to Jamaica each time to get her and sometimes even fly back with her. She would always say that if someone would move to a warmer climate, she would move there and she would stop traveling. That "someone" usually meant me. My mother was diagnosed with Parkinson's disease and as her caregiver I noticed a slow decline in her condition. She was able to do less and less and had difficulty taking care of herself. She went to live with my sister Jennifer for a while, and then came back to me shortly thereafter. For the last two years of her life, she got worse. Those days were physically hard for me. I had a job with demanding expectations and an uncompassionate boss. I was constantly stressed. I had my mother in daycare so I could still go to work. The schedule was tight and I had no wiggle room. Every morning, I got her up and ready for the bus that would take her to the daycare, then after she was picked up, I got dressed and rushed to work while trying not to be late. At the end of the day, I would repeat the cycle. I had to rush home to meet the bus so they wouldn't have to wait for me to arrive so they could drop her off and continue on their way. This stressful game continued for a while.

Their having to wait was not a problem for me, but embarrassing for my mom feeling as if she were holding up everyone else. I was tired a lot as the routine was grueling. Looking back, I wonder if the stress of it all had in some way become my undoing. In order to cope and relieve the stress, I decided to retire early. Three months after I retired, my mother died.

During the months that followed her death, I was extremely depressed and gaining weight. In my effort to lose the weight I had gained, I chose to go on a raw, green diet. Though this diet may look like my own idea, I believe it was part of God's plan for me because He knew what was ahead for me long before I even had a thought. God knew that I would not have been able to weather the storm that was ahead without His help, so in His love and mercy, He prepared me physically for what was about to sweep me off my feet.

I was doing really well experimenting with all kinds of foods that could be eaten raw. I especially liked finding new raw desserts. I ended up losing forty pounds in the process. With my new-found weight loss, people were interested in what I did to shed the pounds. I started doing raw food seminars, which included the NEWSTART program and even compiled a raw food recipe booklet containing most of the recipes that I used to stay on track with the diet. (NEWSTART is an acronym used to outline the eight basic guidelines for healthy living: nutrition, exercise, water, sunshine, temperance, air, rest, and trust in God.) I was confident that what I was doing was exactly what I needed to do to stay healthy. I lived committed to the raw lifestyle for about three years before I slowly began slacking off.

For about a month, I felt myself getting tired with every activity and because I had slacked off from eating as I was before, I felt I was just getting out of shape and that I was experiencing the results of eating dead foods. I had started cooking again and was keeping up with drinking my barley grass juice every morning and walking as often as I could, sometimes three or four times per week and a few extra minutes every day with my dog, but I was certainly not as conscientious as I had been prior. I now lacked the discipline it took to keep up the pace of the raw food lifestyle and I felt this was the result or consequence. I even complained to my sister about how ungrateful I felt my body was now.

I should not have been feeling so tired so quickly with simple activity. I had no idea that this was a clue to something big going on inside my body. I then reflected on what the Psalmist said when he said our bodies are "fearfully and wonderfully made." Only the Creator knows what is going on inside any of our bodies. Even though we may feel healthy and strong, we may be one diagnosis away from a catastrophe. Only God knew for sure and I believe He prepared me for the onslaught.

My philosophy then, before my diagnosis, was that cancer could not flourish in an alkaline environment and as long as I was doing my best to make it so, I was fairly confident that I would never have to worry about the diagnosis of the "big C." What a rude awakening.

I must confess that twenty-five years prior to my diagnosis — in the years before I started eating a plant-based diet — I ate meat of some kind every day. It was not whether I was going to eat meat for dinner — it was what kind of meat I would have for dinner. I was, however, careful to stay away from pork and pork products. We had a commercial freezer stored in our basement that got stocked for months at a time so I was never out of meat.

I tried to process everything but did not have the capacity to do so. I felt blindsided and knocked off of my feet. I still felt sad, depressed at times, anxious, fearful, and lonely all rolled into one. How could I make sense of it all? My life as I knew it was over. Everything was falling apart. What do you do in a situation such as this? I turned to the scriptures for answers, because in them I felt I could gain a better perspective as well as truth to guide me as I faced a situation that was well beyond my comprehension. I found Psalm 34:19 that says, "Many are the afflictions of the righteous." I believed that as long as we are called by the name of Christ, we should expect to go through tribulations which would therefore include adversity and attacks from the enemy in the form of pain and suffering. Then I asked, could it have been the meat I had been eating for all of those years, and is this just a consequence of my choices? I wondered if that had anything to do with my diagnosis. If so, why did it take so long to manifest itself?

In trying to make sense of this, I remembered that in my late twenties, I worked in an industrial lab where I used benzene and acetone on a frequent basis and wondered too if that may be responsible for this dreaded diagnosis. I was looking for anything that could explain the reason for this illness. One doctor said that often when they see cases as mine they are usually caused from exposure to chemicals like benzene. Bingo! I thought this could be my logical answer, but what difference would it make now? I have the disease and nothing was going to change that.

I talked with God, struggled with God, reasoned with God, and complained to God, trying to make sense of what had come upon me. I felt God must have had a hand in this, and He had not dealt with me as I expected Him. I reminded Him that I was His child and that I had been doing so much for the cause of the kingdom.

I was the Personal Ministry leader at my church, promoting and encouraging evangelism and also served as a Sabbath School Superintendent. I went to the women's jail in Indian River County every Wednesday where

I mentored women and shared with them the love of Christ and to the men's prison in Brevard County, two Saturdays each month, as well as volunteering at the prison ministry thrift shop two days each week. In addition to that, I was singing in the choir and on the praise team on Sabbaths and served in the treasury department as a treasury aide. How could He allow this to come upon me when I was doing all good things that I felt He wanted me to do? It was all service to others, which I felt He expects from us. I remembered my mother quoting Exodus 15:26: "If thou wilt diligently hearken to the voice of the Lord thy God, and do what is right in His sight, that He will cause none of these diseases to come upon [*me*]" which He brought upon the Egyptians, so why did this happen to me?

After thinking it over and talking unceasingly to God, I started to internalize my questions and thought, *could it be that I have been so busy doing what I thought God wanted me to do that I didn't have real time for Him?* Was I so consumed with the matters of life that I didn't give God the time He needed? The mere fact that I was angry with God was proof that I didn't know Him as well as I thought. I had what one could call an "aha moment" (or a revelation if you will) regarding my faith. After all my years of going to church and leading out in so many departments, it was entirely possible that my relationship with God was more of an acquaintance with God. Yes, I knew He died to save me; I knew He forgave me of my sins when I asked for forgiveness, so how could I doubt He would take me through this? I did read the Bible, but how? I read so I could gain information for whatever I had to do that day. I read for ideas for a Sabbath school program. I would read to learn how to live a good Christian life; I would read to help me with my presentation to the prisoners at the jail, or when I just needed to deal with a bad situation. Fundamentally, there was nothing wrong with that, but I believe that in my pursuits, I missed the true character of God. In order to trust Him, I had to know Him. I realized that being acquaintances with God would not be enough. I needed a deeper relationship with Him to make it through this storm. It was easy to quote scriptures as a means to an end, but what does it really mean to me in my current situation? I knew the word, but what I needed now was to spend more time with God and seek Him in constant prayer so I could develop a stronger relationship with Him.

I am not trying to make excuses, but when we have been Christians for a long time, we become more involved in the religion of being a Christian than maintaining an intimate relationship with Christ. As a result we lose our grasp on what is real. I became convinced that if I really knew God, I would not have asked as many questions as I did, but would have accepted the fact that God is good, He loves me enough to give His Son for me, and that none of this was His fault.

Friends don't wait for a crisis such as mine to get to know God more deeply. When Jesus broke away from His disciples to a solitary place, it was not to get away from them, but to spend time with His Father from whom He gained His strength. Get to know Jesus more intimately in order to weather any storm that is ahead for you. Someone said, "If you are not in a storm, you are heading into one, so be prepared." I have gone through a lot of thinking, reasoning, and internalizing in order to get the answers and to understand what has taken place with me, when all I needed was a closer relationship with God. Only God knew the answers, the reason or the purpose for this illness and I needed to trust Him not just in words. I needed to truly believe that He would do what He said He would do. I never read the Word as much as I did after I got sick. I now had more than enough time to spare. So I continued to turn to the scriptures for answers and encouragement as I continue to try to make sense of the situation.

I remember talking with Pastor Wintley Phipps on the phone just after he found out I was in the hospital. What he said, paraphrased, is that Satan had to pass through God to get to me, and God allowed only what He knew I could handle. What he said squared up nicely with what Jeremiah said in Lamentations 3:37 (Clear Word),"No one can make anything happen unless the Lord allows it."

Frank Phillips says in his book *His Robe or Mine:*

"Our work is to submit to our life experiences without complaint, accepting everything as coming from Christ, even though it may be coming from Satan. Because Christ's robe of righteousness surrounds us, we must recognize that nothing can touch us except by His permission. (Roman 8:28) Christ permits to touch us only that which will help our character to become like His."

Lamentations 3: 33 says, "But though He causes grief, yet will He have compassion according to the multitude of His mercies. For He doth not afflict willingly, nor grieve the children of men." God does not willingly bring grief to His children.

Then I thought about Jeremiah 29:11-13 (KJV) that says:

> "For I know the thoughts that I think toward you, saith the Lord, thoughts of peace and not of evil, to give you an expected end. Then shall ye call upon me, and ye shall pray unto me, and I will hearken unto you. And ye shall seek me and find me, when ye shall search for me with all your heart."

I felt so much stronger and encouraged after reading these verses. I was now confident that whatever the reason for this disaster, I could rest and be secure in knowing that I had a God who would not willingly bring me grief. I had a God who was waiting for me to call upon Him, and a God who wants only the best for me, His child. I had a feeling of relief knowing that whatever I had to go through, I would be comforted by a Savior who knew what I was going through and was willing to assist me if I only ask Him. I was in a battle for my life, with a deadly killer: leukemia. I needed to understand that going through this did not mean that God had abandoned me. I just had to understand that He was leading behind the scenes and ever-working on my behalf. I needed to be in constant prayer, I needed to be committed to God's will and trust that all things would work together for good of those that love Him. I believed that God would keep His promises, and in all this, He would bring me through even my worst moments. I was going to beat this thing.

One would think that after all the assurances from the Bible that would be the end of that, but no, I kept questioning God. I just felt that because God knew everything, I could confidently go to Him with all my questions and my concerns, and He would never be tired of me. All I could see was my present, but God could see the whole picture and He could see my future. I finally accepted that like Job, I did not deserve an explanation. My only choice was to trust that God knew best and that somehow He would be glorified in the end.

This illness has changed my life in some significant ways. First, it has drawn me closer to God who has become the only constant in my life. In spite of the fact that I felt closer to God now more than ever before, I still had to admit that this illness had caused me to notice more keenly every sign of disease, which in turn has caused me to contemplate that my dying might be imminent. So how does one react in the face of this impending crisis? I struggled daily to find peace in my situation. Trying to keep the faith was hard. Nevertheless, I developed a new relationship with Christ, which gave me peace that all would be well. John 16:33 (KJV) says, "These things I have spoken to you, that in me you might have peace. In this world you shall have tribulation [trouble], but be of good cheer; I have overcome the world."

What I had to go through may have been a plan of the enemy, but I knew that his power was limited to only what God allowed, so I was at peace with the outcome. I was confident that in everything taking place, God would bring something good and give me a platform from which I could give glory to Him.

The next way my life was changed is simply this: I no longer worried about the small things. As someone once said, "Don't sweat the small stuff," I no longer worry about things I cannot control. If it's not in my sphere of responsibility, I immediately turn it over to God. I am inadequate to deal with things that only God can fix. This is when I invoke the serenity prayer. *"God grant me the serenity to accept the things I cannot change; courage to change the things I can; and wisdom to know the difference."*

I realized that God had the last word and because I knew He loved me with an everlasting love and I knew His plan was not to harm me, but to give me hope and a future, I could rest and remain secure in Him. I won't say I wasn't scared of what would happen next, but I had to learn and grow, and I believe I did. Thank God for His mercy and grace.

MY JOURNAL

After being in the hospital in Tampa for a few weeks, a group of ladies from the church came to visit. After relating my experiences to them, one of the ladies asked if I was documenting the events of my time there and I admitted I was not and she encouraged me to start keeping a journal.

Journaling was new to me. I did not like writing my thoughts down for others to read. I think it was just my desire to always be in control. I felt that for my own protection, I should avoid writing things down. I was quite resistant to doing this but later agreed, thinking this could be helpful to someone else. Even then I felt I needed to be careful what I wrote. The young lady encouraged me to write even a few lines each day, and a few lines appealed to me, so I began and these are my best efforts for the days that followed.

Prior to their visit, I had had my first round of chemotherapy and was patiently waiting to see what my bone
marrow would do. At this point, my white cell count was
down to 0.02 — exactly what the chemotherapy was
intended to do. Understandably, there was great concern
about infection since with such a low white cell count, I
now had no protection. I received antibiotics constantly,
and because my bone marrow was not responding as we
expected, my red cell count was also down so I needed
transfusion of red cells as well as platelets frequently.
Here are the entries starting in mid September.

September 17, 2012

*This morning the nurse came in with news that I needed
two units of blood. Not a good way to start the day. I
was not happy because it seemed I was going backward
and not forward. I was terribly discouraged. When the
team of doctors came in to see me, they asked me what
was wrong since I wasn't my old bubbly/chipper self. I
again voiced that I was discouraged. The main doctor
wanted to know why. I explained I have been doing
everything I was supposed to do in eating right, yet this*

came upon me. I was really beginning to feel sorry for myself. He promptly replied, "You did well! That's why you don't have complications from the chemotherapy." I felt so ashamed. When they left, I asked God to forgive me for complaining that things weren't moving fast enough, instead of saying thanks for sparing me from the complications. God is so good. So good He does not treat us as we deserve.

September 21, 2012 – Friday

Still here! Not sure why my cells are not being replenished as expected. I suspect a break in the chemotherapy protocol may be the reason for this. Instead of seven days back-to-back, twenty-four hours per day, my protocol extended to nine days with no account for why that happened. This became a problem for me because now I had to have two bone marrow biopsies instead of one, and they still are not sure of what the results mean. So here I am looking at another bone marrow biopsy and possibly more chemotherapy after being here for twenty-one days already. It is most disconcerting that no one takes responsibility but everyone makes an effort to explain the discrepancy away. I feel like I am just an experiment and the team approach to my treatment just a teaching tool. Not a very good feeling. I understand this is a teaching institution but it's not the way to go for some patients. The team approach allows for a rotation of personnel. Every two weeks there is a new team member and the lead doctor changes every month. When the members of the team change and a new person comes on that is completely unfamiliar with everything, there is no continuity. I have to explain again what I did to the last two individuals. They are basically starting from scratch. It doesn't give me a warm fuzzy feeling at all.

September 22, 2012

My daughter Donna gave me a laptop so I can communicate with emails, etc. Today is Sabbath and I am feeling fine and going to church in Atlanta at the Berea church or in California — wherever Dr. Carlton Byrd is preaching a sermon on <u>the truth about suffering</u>.

His sermon is based on 1 Peter 4:12. I am interested in the subject because I still don't understand this at all. Hopefully I will be encouraged by what he has to say. I was listening so intently that I did not get it all to write it down but I know he said, "You may be suffering now in order to enjoy the future." He also said that suffering brings to us the ministry of the Holy Spirit and our suffering allows us to bless God's holy name and that every time we praise God, it makes Satan nervous. He said we should constantly rejoice because the glory of God is resting on us. He said that when God puts His people through fiery trials, He keeps His eye on the clock and His hands on the thermostat. He determines how hot and for how long. He encouraged me to rest in God since He has the last word. Makes sense to me.

The song for special music is "How Many Times" by the Brooklyn Tabernacle.

How many times must I prove how much I love you
How many ways must my love for you I show
How many times must I rescue you from trouble
For you to know just how much I love you

CHORUS
Didn't I wake you up this morning
Were you clothed in your right mind

When you walked on this problem
Didn't I step right in on time
When you got weak along life's journey
My angel carried you
So you would know just how much I love you

VERSE 2
How many days must I be fence all around you
How many nights must I wipe your tears away
How many storms must I bring you safely through
For you to know just how much I love you

CHORUS 2
Didn't I put food on your able
Show UP! when your bills were due
When the pains were racking your body
Didn't I send healing down to you
When you were lost in sin and sorrow
I died to set you free
So you would know just how much I love you

I viewed several sermons today. I had a really good day!

Another one is: "Check your roots" *The song:* "The Battle is not yours." *He says that when Satan attacks you, it will show your spiritual depth. We should say as Job, "Though He slays me, yet will I trust Him." He asked us to remember the verse that conveys the thought, "God did not bring you this far to leave you." He said that though we can't see far, we can take one step at a time to make it to our destination. God promises to bless you so take one step at a time because you may be just one step from your breakthrough.*

The Battle is not yours
Written by Michael McKay

There is no pain what Jesus can't feel, There is no hurt, He cannot heal
All things work according to His perfect will, No matter, what you're going through
Remember God is only using You, For the battle is not yours
It's the Lord's

There's no sadness Jesus can't feel, And there is no sorrow
That He cannot heal, For all things work, according to
the Master's holy will,
No matter what you're going through, Remember that
God is only using You
For the battle is not yours, It's the Lord's

No matter what, You're going through
Remember that God, Only wants to use you
For the battle is not yours, It's the Lord's

No matter what, You happen to go through right now
Remember that in the midst of it all, God only wants to
use you
No matter what you're going through
For the battle is not yours, It's the Lord's

No matter what it is, that you're going through
Hold your head up, stick your chest out
And remember He's using you
No matter what you're going through
God is only using you

For this battle is not yours alone, This battle is not yours, no
You cannot handle it all by yourself
No, no, no, no, no, no, It's not yours
This battle is not yours, It's the Lord's, not yours

This battle is not yours, The Lord is the only one who can fight it
He wants to use you as His vessel, So be open to Him, It's not yours
No It's not yours, It's the Lord's

The other one is: "Will the real you please stand up?" *I was listening so intently I was not able to write anything down. Special music was: God is (the joy and the strength of my life). I enjoyed all the music today. They ministered to my soul while taking me far away from here, living in this dreary place for so many days.*

God Is – Rev. James Cleveland

God is the joy and the strength of my life,
He moves all pain, misery, and strife.

He promised to keep me, never to leave me.
He's never ever come short of His word.

I've got to fast and pray, stay in His narrow way,
I've got to keep my life clean everyday;
I want to go with Him when He comes back,
I've come too far and I'll never turn back.

God is (8x), God is my all in all.

September 23, 2012

I am still here. The nurses are excited about the little increase in WBC from 0.02 to 0.26–0.37. Not knowing what to expect by way of recovery, I got excited too, just thankful for small mercies. I have a biopsy tomorrow and I'm still looking for a miracle to occur overnight so they will cancel the biopsy.

Tricia is leaving today. She has to pick up Valerie from Mt. Calvary SDA church where she is attending with Michelle some Obama initiative. I hope she finds the church and gets to the airport on time. I would hate to think of how we would get my car back here in Tampa from the airport in Orlando if she does not find the address of the church in time. Also how would Valerie get around here without the car? I don't want to think about it. Nothing I can do from my hospital bed anyway. Stop worrying.

I guess I am concerned about how I am going to adjust to life alone again in my room for however long I continue to be here. I just can't imagine how Tricia could tolerate being in a hospital room for so long without being sick. I am really going to miss her and the companionship.

She tried so hard to get me the greens we thought would help my white cell count to come back to normal. I'm scared they may not have washed the greens well before juicing. I have a low-grade fever and diarrhea but I am afraid to say I had the greens, because they don't want me to have any fruit or vegetable except from the kitchen because I am Neutropenic. I am really nervous about what this means right now.

September 24, 2012

I am supposed to have my third biopsy today and I am scared of what they will find. I am concerned about having even more chemotherapy. I try to encourage myself with music.

My song today is by the Brooklyn Tabernacle:

You don't have to worry and don't you be afraid.
Joy comes in the morning, troubles they don't last always.
For there's a friend in Jesus who will wipe your tears away
And if your heart is broken just lift your hands and say

Chorus: For I know that I can make it I know that I can stand,
No matter what may come my way; my life is in your hands.
With Jesus I can take it with Him I know I can stand,
No matter what may come my way; my life is in your hands.

When your test and trials they seem to get you down,

And all your friends and loved ones are nowhere to be found.

Remember there's a friend in Jesus, Who will wipe your tears away

And if your heart is broken just lift your hands and say.

I am thankful for this encouragement because I have to get ready for this biopsy and I am not ready for the outcome. Today, not only do I have to have the biopsy, but I am NPO (nothing by mouth) from midnight and just found out that I will be the last patient on the list to be seen today because of my diagnosis of Clostridium Difficile (C. Diff). I should have been seen before the outpatients but had to wait until 2:00 p.m. when the room was cleared. You see they did not want me in the exam and procedure area until they were done with all the other patients because it would mean major clean up after me for them to see other patients. C.Diff. is contagious. I really right now feel like a leper needing to call out unclean. The signs were posted for special precaution so there was no need to say it. Everyone had to wear special gowns, mask and gloves to enter the preparation room.

I continue to ask God why! Why me? Why now? What am I to learn from this? If I have to have a second round of chemotherapy, will that bring glory to Him? How do I overcome the pressing desire to feel sorry for myself and just give up? Where is He in the middle of this situation? I feel so alone right now. I just don't sense His presence with me and there is this overwhelming feeling of emptiness. It was then I thought about Job and what he went through, but I could not equate myself with Job, except that I had no idea why I was in this situation, but I'm no Job so what gives? I am so full of questions with no answers. I tried reading excerpts from the book of Job. I focused on chapter 12:9 and that said, "All nature knows that the Lord made all things and that He is still in control. The life of every living thing is in His hand as is the breath of every creature." I am thinking it's up to Him to save my life or take it. I was in a sad state.

Then in reading I came across Psalm 39. I felt guilty and convicted after reading verse nine in the Clear Word version that says, "I will keep quiet and not complain *about my circumstances. You could have prevented these things from happening, but I will trust your wisdom."*

I asked God for forgiveness for not trusting Him.

September 25, 2012 – Day 36

I had a biopsy and just waiting to hear the results. It will be quite interesting to see what happens. This has been quite a journey so far. I am obviously disappointed since my last day of chemotherapy was August 29th. I believe a series of missteps led me to now four weeks out with no positive results. My white cells are not regenerating as they should and no one knows what the next day will bring. I got up to do my devotions such as it is these days, and I found a reading perfect for my situation. Suddenly I felt that God knew ahead of time that I would need this today. I have been asking all these why's and all I can think about today is that Jesus when going to the cross asked His father to remove the cup if at all possible. I had asked that if possible, that I would not have to have the chemotherapy a second time, but His will be done. Peter 4:12-16.

I am feeling a bit guilty that I should not question God, but I feel that if we have a relationship with Him as a friend there should be nothing wrong with talking with Him in trying to understand, whatever the situation might be. Right now I am anxious and another round of chemotherapy is not what I would choose to have done if I had the choice. I have always thought of God as a personal God who know our needs and understands our thoughts. So why feel guilty to ask if He already knows what I am thinking? I honestly don't feel strong enough to go through it again.

I truly believe that because of my pride in what I thought I did to make me strong enough to go through it the first time with little or no complications, I was not giving God the credit, I now have to go through it again from a point of weakness so that God only will get the glory when I come out on the other side of this ordeal. My mantra now is, "If it is to be it's not up to me." I have somehow been able to surrender to God's will without giving up hope. Thank God for that.

September 26, 2012

I was told yesterday that I had to have a new round of chemotherapy with only a fifty percent chance of recovery. Not good odds even for a gambling person. The thing I feared most has come upon me. I am not sure if after thirty-six days here with no result that I can handle another round of chemotherapy and twenty-eight more days of confinement. Before starting this process, I did not have a good grasp of my situation. I thought that once I had chemo and came to remission I would be fine and that would be that. How naïve. The fifty percent idea was beginning to sink in and wearing on me heavily. It was beginning to sink in that my odds were not good and even the doctors were telling me ahead of time not to expect too much. This disclaimer was having a terrible effect on me. Prior to today, I did not really understand that the day of my diagnosis was the end of my life as I knew it. I was slowly slipping down into a pit of despair. The thought that I would get the chemotherapy, possibly get sick as a side effect, recover, and go home was now out of the question. It did not help to hear a nurse discussing in my presence why he liked working in the area of end-of-life.

My friend and neighbor Mae called today and I expressed my realization and the odds the doctor gave me. She promptly asked me, "Whose report will you believe? If you give up now, you are in agreement that it's over." I have to remember that God is in control, He is in charge of our lives and can operate outside the odds. Because He is all powerful, nothing is too hard for Him. Regardless of our circumstances or seemingly impossible situations, He promises He will be with us. Although I gave it a lot of thought, I am still having difficulty getting out of bed.

I don't want to get out of bed and I don't want to talk to anyone today. I just want to spend some time contemplating my odds while trying to decide if I want to do another round of chemotherapy. One nurse remarked that the doctor who gave me those odds was unsympathetic in the way he told me the facts, and that honesty without compassion is brutality. I felt that was quite brutal because I felt even worse after that conversation.

The pharmacist came to my room to explain what would be done with this round of chemotherapy.

Recognizing that I had not accomplished what I expected and feeling that I had no other option, I agreed to the chemotherapy and signed the consent form then I went straight to bed and drew the covers over my head.

I will start chemo tonight, whatever the odds. Earlier I decided if it was to be it was not up to me, so regardless of the odds, it was no longer my responsibility. All I had to do now was to submit and allow God to handle it. I was no longer in control, as if I ever was.

September 27, 2012

I started chemo last night with a shot of Neupogen in the gut after quite a struggle to get the drug as prescribed. I was made aware of the fact that they had planned to substitute the drug for a generic form without informing me. I refused to have the procedure without the drug that was offered on the consent form. When I questioned the switch I was told it was a hospital-wide switch for the last three months, but they just offered it to me yesterday. The whole thing was attributed to the individual preparing the consent form not writing in the new drug. I questioned the difference in the drugs but did not get a straight-forward answer. I then mentioned that I had a brother who was a pharmacist and I would call while they wait to get the answer. The pharmacist immediately agreed that they had a small supply available that they could use and that ended the saga of the Neupogen shots. I did not want another reason for this round of chemotherapy to fail. It took quite a while for me to agonize over the decision before agreeing to subject my body to another round. I felt they failed in the first round because of errors in dispensing the drug and I wanted no more mistakes on this one especially with the fifty/ fifty odds.

Today I started with another shot in the gut then the chemo an hour later. The shot as I understand it, is to wake up the Leukemia cells and move them out of the bone marrow so the chemo drug can kill them.

It's 1:25 on day two of six days of chemotherapy and I am beginning to feel the nausea coming on. I found Psalm 77 that describes exactly how I felt yesterday.

September 28, 2012

I survived day three of chemotherapy so far and had a decent day today. I left the room to sit at the window overlooking the rock garden. Did a whole fill-in puzzle. Nausea reigns. I had to get Ativan before going to bed but tomorrow is another day. I gave the folks in the kitchen my juicer and got my first fresh carrot juice today, it was pretty good. I got too much food and I can't eat much because of the nausea. I am so sick. God help me.

September 29, 2012

I got up this morning with nausea. I'm ready with the bucket but hate to do it. Lord please help me.

Bill is my nurse and offered to give me IV Zofran. It helped somewhat, so at least I can eat before starting day four of chemotherapy. I have been so sick it's beyond description. God provides what we need to sustain us in difficult and trying times. I found this devotional in "Our Daily Bread" to help me through the day:

"When the storms of life hit so hard that we nearly break from the force, our loving father God has allowed it to make us stronger. He uses the water from the storm that batters us on the outside to build us up on the inside so we can stand straight and strong. Never fear, for the storms that threaten to destroy us God will use to strengthen us."

September 30, 2012

Today is day five of my second round of chemotherapy and Bill is my nurse.

It's going to take everything in me to start this day. I have cried and cried out to God for help. All night the tears run warm down my cheeks. I need to know He is here with me. I feel so alone. I ask for forgiveness for anything I have done that would bring this on me. Just as I am crying asking, "God where are you?" and reminding Him that He promised He would never leave me or forsake me, but I don't feel Him near. As if God were answering me, my friend Juanita called to say she is thinking about me. While I am crying and describing to Juanita how awful I felt during the night that had passed, Bill came into the room, kneeled on the floor next to my bed and started rubbing my arm.

After Juanita prayed with me, I was able to get out of bed and read a psalm or two. It seems that the nausea has abated somewhat so I can focus if only for a short time. I don't feel like I have it in me to go through another day of chemotherapy and the treatment hasn't even started yet. I am really thankful for Sis. Richard's call because somehow, I got the strength to go through the day. Later Sis Mavis called and prayed with me. I honestly believe that the sincere prayer of a righteous man availeth much. My song today is, "Precious Lord take my hand lead me on help me stand, I'm tired I'm weak I'm worn." I really didn't think I was going to make it through that day.

Another amazing thing about today that showed me God is responding to my cry for help is that Bill my nurse, after setting up everything for the treatment and double checking that everything was in place, said to me, "One more thing Ms. Arline," then he came over to where I was sitting and gave me a big bear hug. I do in fact believe God was showing me that He was indeed with me. He sent Bill, Mavis and Juanita. I thank you God for Your assurance just when I needed it.

I found a poem on God's care and provision suitable for the moment. It was written by Helen Steiner Rice and given to me by a friend who was trying to encourage me.

Is the Cross You Wear Too Heavy to Bear? (Helen Steiner Rice)

Complainingly I told myself this cross was too heavy to wear,
And I wondered discontentedly why God gave it to me to bear.
I looked with envy at others who crosses seemed lighter than mine
and wished that I could change my cross for one of a lighter design.
Then in a dream I beheld the cross I impulsively wanted to wear –
It was fashioned of pearls and diamonds and gems that are precious and rare,
and when I hung it around my neck,

The weight of the jewels and the gold
Was much too heavy and cumbersome
So I tossed it aside, and before my eyes was a cross of
rose-red flowers
This cross I can wear for hours, so lovely and light
and thin
But I had forgotten about the thorns that started to
pierce my skin

Then in a dream I saw my cross rugged and old
and plain
The clumsy old cross I had looked upon with discon-
tented disdain
And at last I knew that God had made this special
cross for me
For God in His great wisdom knew what I before could
not see
That often the loveliest crosses are the heaviest crosses
to bear
For only God is wise enough to choose the cross each
can wear
For your cross has been blessed

God made it just for you to wear and remember God knows best.

October 1, 2012

This is day six of my second round of chemotherapy

I have been sick all day and haven't had much of anything to eat because I am afraid to throw up. This is the last day and it seems to be worse than all the others. They have been trying combinations of drugs to help me with the nausea but nothing is working right now.

My sister Valerie is here with me. We should have been discharged since September 18th but she is still here today (Oct. 1), waiting for another round of chemo to be completed so she can take me home. She was concerned about my not eating, so she tried to assist me with my meal dilemma. She purchased a fruit smoothie for me to replace dinner since my tray was taken while I was asleep. She bought two smoothies at almost $5.00 each, and ended up spilling one. To make things worse, I could only complete half of the one she gave me before I was feeling full and nauseous. This has been a rough day.

While my sister Valerie was with me, she was able to spend all that time at the home of a friend Michelle, someone she'd never met and someone who came to visit me and offered to help me in any way she could. Little did I know it would turn out to be accommodation for my family at her home and for such an extended period of time. Michelle is the daughter of Mellani and Ken, members from my church in Palm Bay, Florida. This was certainly a blessing because we had no idea how long Valerie would need to remain there with Michelle but she was so open and generous with her invitation. I know that God worked that out for us even before we knew there had to be a second round of chemotherapy. My sister passed the time reading from her Kindle and playing golf when she could. We are extremely thankful to Michelle for her generosity and love, and to God for His provision.

October 2, 2012

I am feeling really sick and think I am just going to die. I have nausea around the clock; I don't seem to get a break, and to top it off, the pulmonary medicine department wants me to sign consent to do a bronchos-copy tomorrow. They want to know what type of fungus I have growing on my lungs and felt this was just as good a time as any to do the surgery. I don't want to do it but I am just too weak to argue about it. I asked the doctor they sent to my room, if it was possible to get a break in time before doing another procedure since I had just completed a second round of chemotherapy and did not feel up to doing this. My sister tried to bargain with them for another day before trying to perform another procedure. This, they claim, was the only time available. The doctor just looked at me stone-faced as if to say, "And?" I said I would think about it and let them know. I asked them to leave the consent form and I would sign it when I decided what I wanted to do. From the excuses they made, it was evident that they had already made the decision and I was already scheduled for the pro-cedure. It was just a matter of convincing me of how important it was to have the procedure done.

October 3, 2012

I must explain that at admission to the cancer center, I was found to have mold on my lung and was being treated by the infectious disease department.

Now I feel I have to cooperate with the plan, but I am just too weak to go through it just to find out what type of fungus I had growing there.

I got up early this morning and started my day today NPO (nothing by mouth) because they really expected me to have this procedure today. I felt I had to do it, but I believe the Holy Spirit intervened. As I was preparing for my day, I clearly heard a voice asking me why I was doing it. I answered, "I don't know," as if someone was in the room with me. The voice said, "don't do it." Somehow I got the strength to respond and defend my reason for not wanting the procedure done. An hour after responding to the voice I heard, a doctor from the pulmonary department came in to pick up the signed consent for the bronchoscopy. I told her I did not sign it because I did not have the strength to read it. I never knew someone could be so weak.

I explained that I felt I did not have a choice and she said I did. I told her if I did have a choice, I don't want to have the procedure done and for a number of reasons, greatest of which is the fact that I was too weak right now and it had only been one day after chemotherapy. I explained that I did not consider the procedure to be an emergency; I was not coughing so there was no fear of droplet infection. I did not have colored sputum, rattles, or rales and my blood count was still too low to attempt anything so risky.

She left without me signing the form, but not long after, there was a literal parade of doctors trying to convince me that I needed the procedure. After several attempts to convince me, they conceded and I did not have the procedure.

I had a wonderful day. I was able to walk around the halls without difficulty. I believe not having medication today may have something to do with it. Since I was NPO, I had nothing to bog me down.

I found out later that they were not supposed to operate on anyone with a platelet count of less than fifty. My count was only twenty-nine. If I got a nick, I could bleed out because I did not have enough clotting agents in my blood stream.

I also found the type of fungus I had on my lung without the procedure.

God is awesome. I unexpectedly had a temperature of one hundred and two degrees and the protocol in this situation required a blood culture, which was done. In the report that followed the test, they discovered that I had aspergillosis, a fungus found in dead leaves and rotting wood products found in any yard and if my immune system was not compromised I could have fought it off with no problem. We got the answer without the bronchoscopy. I only got the information because a nurse who read the report decided to let me know. The hospital did not give me a copy of the report I guess because it would mean admitting the procedure was totally unnecessary.

The procedure involved making an incision in the neck as they explained it to me, and they promise to "numb you up real good" and then enter to spray water to wash the fungus, extract the fluid and culture it to see what was growing there. Thank God for intervening on my behalf. The ramification could be astounding.

The thought of having the procedure done and having any fluid left behind is unthinkable. I picture myself on oxygen for the rest of my life because of fluid on my lungs as well as difficulty breathing due to fluid left behind. I just thank God for speaking to me that morning and for giving me the strength to stand fast. Praise God.

October 4 & 5, 2012

Nothing today I am too sick to even think straight.

October 6, 2012

I had no desire to write anything for the last few days; I just felt too sick. I stayed in bed all day. Actually, I stayed in bed for twenty-four hours eating little or nothing. Miss Phoebe and Everton came to visit early in the day, then Brother and Sister Gomes came to visit later. They felt so sorry for my sister Valerie having to purchase her meals everyday that they left her a card with money to assist her with meals as she stayed at the hospital for so long.

My PICC line for administering medication is clogged and all efforts to unclog it even with clot buster drugs seem to be of no avail. The nurse on duty did not seem very competent which made me nervous. She had notes scribbled on what to do next. She was unsuccessful in getting the line unclogged and the hours are slipping by. It was already 4:00 p.m. with no IV medications. She suggested that she would have to start an IV to administer the meds if she was not able to clear the line. The problem is she had to give me potassium and there was no way for her to do that through a peripheral IV. I am not sure she even thought about that.

Once my sister heard her say she wanted to start an IV, she decided we had waited long enough and we needed to pray about this matter. We prayed asking God to intervene in this situation. Because we had no confidence in the nurse's ability, we could only envision the worst. After praying, another nurse came into my room to find out what was going on. Like a nurse on a mission, she decided to try to unclog the line. In no time, whatever she did — or rather, God did — the line was clear and I could finally get my medications. Thank God for His mercies. I am learning to see them now. He is always faithful. Psalm 121 says, "I will lift up my eyes to the hills, where does my help come from? My help comes from the Lord who makes heaven and earth."

October 7, 2012 (Sunday)

I got up determined to get out of the hospital gown today. I tried to shower and change, but I still feel so weak. Thank God I got it done.

My devotion was Psalm 46. "Be still and know that I am God." Put your hands down and allow God to work for you. I had a hard time trying to decide what constituted putting my hands down. I had to learn to stop striving and let God intervene in my situation without my interference.

This was difficult for me because I always felt I had to fix things. Still having difficulty with letting go and letting God even though I know He is in control. Why is it so hard? For years I have been able to create an illusion of strength and self-sufficiency, but when cancer hit I had to learn that my total dependence should be in God. I needed to stop struggling and wait for God to do His work. I have a long way to go to move into this deeper relationship of faith and trust in God and God alone and not in my own self-reliance. I believe He was just waiting for me to let go so He could function. The sooner I got there, the better it would be for me. I needed to be able to wait patiently and prayerfully for His deliverance instead of chafing at the neck struggling to make things happen on my own.

This was my song for the day: "God is our refuge and strength, a very present help in time of trouble, He is our refuge and strength, for we know that He is God."

I am finding that I can't just know this in my head; it has to be real in my life even when I can't explain why I feel so sick.

Because I stayed in bed for twenty-four hours yesterday, my back is killing me. The mattress is so very thin. I told my tech and she found a different bed for me with the mattress two times thicker than the one I was sleeping on. God be praised! He provides even when we don't expect it.

October 13, 2012

I haven't written anything for quite a few days because I have been so sick. I go to bed sick and wake up sick. I am just sick around the clock. I am glad I can get up and write again.

Today I am up and writing again because they have decided to give me scheduled doses of the anti-nausea medication, which should help keep me from being so sick all the time.

Here are highlights of the past days as I remember them. On Thursday, Pastor and Mrs. Phipps came to visit. Linda brought me silk flowers from the gift shop and my sister thought they were real. She commenced to tell her I could not have live flowers. It really fooled her and we had a good laugh.

I think the Phipps saw me at my worst. I was crying and there was snot in abundance under my mask which I had to wear whenever I left my room. It was just a pitiful sight. I think I used a box of tissues during the visit. I was pleased to see them and thankful that they took the time to visit with me.

At one of my visits I hugged my visitor which I should not have done. I was not supposed to have contact with anyone even though I was wearing my mask. Last night I spiked a fever of ninety-nine degrees and the next day it moved to one hundred and two degrees. There was a flurry of activity in my room as a result. They did blood cultures taking samples from the pick line and from fresh draw as well as a urine culture. I didn't care for the fresh stick because I hate pain. Thankfully they showed nothing to be concerned about.

My temperature today is one hundred point four degrees. I got Tylenol for the fever and sweated a lot. I hope that meant the fever broke. I would hate to go out this way. They have changed my antibiotics to keep up with whatever it is that broke through their elaborate chemical defenses. We'll just wait and see what comes from this.

During the time I was not able to write, I had visits from members of the Palm Bay Church some transported by Sis Dawn Burch. I thank her so much for brightening up my day and toting others with her to do the same.

I have not been able to eat because of the nausea, so now the dietary department has decided to keep track of what I am eating or not eating so they can justify tube feeding. Can you imagine that? That would be more like adding insult to injury. I have to try to eat more to avoid this drastic move.

October 19, 2012

Today the team came in and the doctor told me they would consider sending me home in five days. I was so excited to think there was indeed light at the end of the tunnel. It couldn't be true, *I thought, because my WBC (white blood cell count) was still only 0.52. I am trusting God now to do as He promised and do some-thing miraculous for me. I had a good day just thinking of the possibility of going home and possibly going to remission. So many times I felt like giving up, but only by God's grace I didn't. I realize it's not by my strength that I will make it. It's all in His hands. I finally sur-rendered. There was nothing I could do. It was all up to Him now. My BP is high, my K+(Potassium) is low, I need platelets because they are low, and I need two bags of packed red cells because my RBC is low. I can't handle it. I decided it's no longer my problem. It's all*

His. I totally surrendered and prayed to keep it that way. I am not in control.

The song "He's Able" comes to my mind as it adequately describes how I feel going through this second series of poison.

God's mercy kept me so I wouldn't let go.

October 20, 2012

This has been a very uneventful day except that I was allowed to go downstairs to the first floor alone. I felt good enough to take some pictures and returned to the floor without incident. On my way I had several people ask if I was leaving today. Is there something I should know? My cell count seem to be inching up which brings me a bit of optimism. Hyacinth, Marjorie, and Hyacinth's in-laws came to visit from Fort Lauderdale/ Pembroke Pines and West Palm. It's been quite a treat. They brought me coconut water — three of which I had before the day was over.

My legs are swollen but no one seems very concerned about it so I guess I shouldn't worry about it either. I am not sure how to take it. The team leader seems to think it's ok.

Yvonne and Philmore should have come by now, not sure what the problem is. She is supposed to be bringing me a small tape recorder to document my journey making it easier for me on the days I don't feel like writing anything.

October 21, 2012

This was a good day! Sis Burch and her caravan of ladies came visiting again. Each time she brings a different group of ladies but she was the constant. I can't imagine driving those miles unless you really cared, so just being here spoke volumes for her.

I feel she had to care very much in order to make the trip twice "across the country" as I like to say about coming from the east coast to the west coast.

My brother and his wife also came today and brought me coconut water and my sister Valerie brought me rice, peas, and curried vegetables.

God has been good to me, but I have been slow to learn the lessons He has been trying to teach me. Isaiah

18:1-5, watching and waiting. It was a pleasure for them as I was able to eat what they brought me we learned a new song from my sister as we sat around talking about how far I had come. The song says: "Look at me I am a testimony." I am certainly a testimony of God's love when sometimes I felt nothing.

> *"Look at me, I'm a testimony, I didn't make it on my own and I'm not standing here alone. It is Jesus who gave me this opportunity; look at me I'm a testimony. It is Jesus who made me a possibility, Jesus who never gave up on me."*

October 22, 2012

I have written nothing for the past week, just not feeling up to it.

I am writing today because this is supposed to be D-Day. Today I am up before the birds. It's 4:30 a.m. and I can't sleep. I am here wondering if I am really going to finally leave here, or if I will be disappointed because my blood cell counts will not be high enough for them to send me home. Anxious to find out, but must wait since everyone is still sleeping. I have decided to let God be God and just go along for the ride. It took a lot to get to this point and I'm asking God to keep me in this place of dependence where everything is His business and the load is off me and squarely on His shoulders. For whatever reason I was dealt this blow, God only knows. How and when it will end is entirely up to Him. I just give Him praise for giving me one more day to make things right with Him.

I was so determined to leave the hospital that day; I kept pressing to have the discharge papers done. No one seemed to be in a hurry to get it done until about late evening. I was packed and waiting ready to go at a moment's notice as if that would change anything if they decided to keep me. I finally left the hospital at about 7:00 p.m, so I stayed at the Wyndham hotel in town. It was too late to take a three hour ride from the west coast of Florida back to Palm Bay and I was just too tired to take the trip that night. I had spent sixty-five days there and I was extremely nervous to be in the outside world without constant medication. I was so afraid something would happen during the night but God kept me and I woke up feeling fine. I was then ready for my trip home, thank you Jesus.

Once I began treatment I was cognizant of the fact that I *could* die as a result of this disease. After the experiences I have had at that facility, I knew I *would* die and not necessarily from this disease, except for the mercy of God who chose to spare my life in spite of my unfaithfulness.

On my way back home from the hospital, I decided my first stop would be the church. I asked my sister Valerie to take me to the Palm Bay Seventh Day Adventist Church, a rather odd request she may have thought, but she agreed. I knew no one would be in the sanctuary during the day, so no one would know what I was doing. I went to the altar (the front of the platform) and I poured out my heart to God thanking Him for His mercy, grace, and faithfulness in bringing me back home. In the silence, I could talk with Him here as my friend who had been with me through sixty-five days of hard trials even through the valley of the shadow of death, and He chose to deliver me.

As the tears streamed warm down my face, I asked God for forgiveness for not trusting Him as I should and forgiveness for the anger and resentment I felt at the diagnosis. Then I thanked Him for the life I have in Him. I praised Him for the new deeper relationship we now had and I thanked Him for being Lord of my life. Even if this journey should end in death, I now accepted it will be according to His timing and His will.

I prayed for strength to carry on to the end of this journey wherever it may lead me. I knelt there for quite a while praying. I don't remember much else of what I said, I felt I had been to a spiritual boot camp and now I was on my way home and sincerely grateful for it.

THE CHEMO EFFECT

*W*hen I started my chemotherapy treatment, the nurses told me I would lose my hair, but the optimist in me said, "No way, not me." One nurse was bold enough to name the day. "By day fourteen," he said, "you will begin losing your hair."

Because he was so specific, I watched with interest to see if he would be right, and sure enough, the hair started coming out in clumps on my pillow without me even touching it. I made arrangements to go to the beauty shop in the hospital and was told that if I had come to cut the hair before it started to come out I might have had a better opportunity of it growing back thicker. I was sorry to hear that because I always had thin hair and would have loved the opportunity to have thick hair for a change. My loss I guess. I was determined I would not wear a wig so I struggled with finding the right hat for church. I have a small head, so with no hair to hold the hat on my head, it was quite a challenge. I tried stuffing the hats with scarves to keep it from falling down over my eyes but that only made the situation worse because the scarves caused the hat to stand up off my head instead and revealed more baldness than I cared to expose. It was funny looking at myself in the mirror with each fitting.

Fortunate for me, my treatment ended at the hospital and I made it home on October 22, 2013. By the time I was able to go out to church, it was well into the fall season so I could wear felt hats that had some sticking ability and I no longer needed the scarves. Losing my hair was by far the most challenging side effect of all and proved to be a trying time that took a little getting used to. Although I did not have long hair prior to my illness, I was able to manage what I had so I would look acceptable. Losing my hair from my head was not the only hair loss I had to contend with; I lost my eye brows and eyelashes, which I believe coupled with the bald head, gave me that classic cancer patient look and to my delight, my under arm no longer needed shaving.

Because the drugs attack both cancer cells and healthy growing cells, the side effects were many.

Not only did I lose all of my hair for a second time, but I also lost muscle mass. It was quite evident when trying to cut produce at home, especially ones with thick skin. In the produce store I often had to ask the attendant to cut my squash or watermelon into four parts for me and wrap them in plastic wrap, because I just did not have the strength to do it myself at home.

Another thing that resulted from the chemo that I had to accept or at least get used to, was the loss of my sense of taste. It made it tough for me to find food to eat because nothing had any taste. I ate because I knew I had to eat and I had a hard time deciding what to eat. My sense of smell was also perverted and I had the hardest time when my sister Valerie (who was my care giver after my return home from my first hospitalization) decided she would cut up onions, green and red peppers early in the morning to prepare for cooking that day. She is an early riser and did her best work in the mornings. I would lose my appetite, which was already almost non-existent. Because of these and other issues, I had to force myself to eat just to get the nutrients in.

While in the first hospital, I was told I needed to eat more because I had started losing weight. To handle the problem, the dietary department began offering me a soy milkshake at every meal to be sure I was getting the nutrients. I felt like cattle fattening up for market. They gave me soymilk in consideration that I was a vegetarian. All those shakes accounted for a lot more calories than I would have eaten if I had the choice. Losing weight was definitely frowned upon.

One more side effect of the chemo was the fact that all nails — hands and feet — had a black hue. I thought at first it was a fungus, so I showed it to my hematologist who promptly informed me it was the chemo. At Christmas, I got a gift certificate for a pedicure and manicure. I forgot about the nail issue until I had to have the work done. I was a bit embarrassed when I saw the darkness but knew I was looking at the poison of the chemo leaving my system so I tried to explain it away. I left the hospital in October, so by January, one would expect that the blackness would be gone but I could still see the line separating the clear and dark areas of my nails.

Next, my skin became so dry, it looked like that of an alligator. It did not matter how much lotion I used, in an hour it would soak in and again looked as if I never did anything to my skin.

I also had a heightened sensitivity to hot and cold. I had to be careful when eating hot foods, not to burn the lining of my mouth, which somehow seemed to be much thinner after the chemo. I tried taking a can of frozen juice from the freezer once and it stuck to my hand. It actually peeled off a part of my skin that had become so thin.

The worst side effect of all, for me, was my diminishing memory. My answer frequently was, "Did I say that"? or, "I don't remember saying that," because I really did not remember. I have difficulty remembering events, names, or dates so I make notes. Sometimes in the middle of a conversation I would forget what I was trying to say and had to wait for the thought to come back to me.

In my first occurrence while in Tampa, one hour before each chemotherapy treatment, I was given a white blood cell stimulating shot called neupogen. I was given that drug in order to bring the faulty cells from the bone marrow so they could be wiped out. I was told it caused severe muscle and joint pains in some people, but I never experienced it. After the relapse, I was given the same drug after chemo treatment. This time, it was given to speed up the recovery of the white cell count and it was then that I had problems with severe bone pain.

There were folks with sores in their esophagus who were unable to or had difficulty swallowing, sores on the palms of their hands, and other situations. I thank God I did not experience as many complications as I could have. I believe that God protected me and for that I am so grateful. I believe the prayers of the saints had a lot to do with my outcome.

I experienced tiredness and a low energy level. I struggled with stomach issues and terrible nausea that even the medication did not seem to help. I was so weak at the end of each treatment that I could not decide which I hated more, weakness or nausea. One day I broke down crying, I couldn't believe someone could be so weak and I had no idea how to make it better.

At times during chemotherapy, mostly at night, I felt as though all my teeth were falling from their sockets. That was definitely a weird feeling. I would get up in the morning and check to see if they were still there in my mouth. The one thing I knew for sure during my ordeal was that it could have been so easy to give up but for the grace of God.

What I Discovered about Family, Food and Friends

Family

I have a small family and because of the number of times I had to be in and out of the hospital, I quickly found out that cancer affects the whole family, not just the individual with the disease. Many lives are changed because of this one diagnosis. Fortunately for me, my son was with me when I first went to the emergency room and within a short time one of my daughters was in the hospital with me where we found out the diagnosis together. I can't say I know how they are dealing with it because I don't think they want me to worry about it. It's a heavy load for young adults with active lives. I had to accept that they have their own lives and responsibilities and could not always be there. I may have wanted them to spend a lot of time with me but I also knew they had jobs and young families of their own. I still, however, depend on them for emotional support and leaned heavily on my siblings. I found it was easy to talk to them about my condition and they were always ready to help. The problem I had was having everyone adjust his or her own lives because of me. When I was first diagnosed, I felt that everyone went to extreme measures to take care of me. I felt a certain amount of guilt for having them spend so much of their time and resources because of me. It was hard to accept the fact that what they were doing was what they wanted to do for me and all I had to do was to accept it gracefully.

The most important things I've learned from my experiences with this blood cancer over the years, is how critical it is to have family and friends and also how powerful it is to have a praying group of people — my church family — in my corner.

Food

This is a tricky subject for many, because it depends on one's like or dislikes when it comes to food. I can only tell you what I personally did to survive.

It is not unusual for individuals with Leukemia to have questions about what foods to eat during and after treatment. I never knew what I wanted to eat. I would decide on something and by the time I got it, I no longer wanted it. Although I got a lot of advice on what I should eat to overcome my cancer, it is important to note that there is no specific food or special diet that has been proven to control cancer. Because of individual nutritional needs, it's best to have a talk with your doctor about what foods you should be eating.

During my treatment, I was mostly neutropenic (low white blood cells), so raw fruits and vegetables were not recommended. My rule of thumb for eating fresh fruits during treatment, with my doctor's approval, was if the fruit has a hard shell or thick skin, I could have it. I just had to make sure someone else washed it and peeled it for me. Later I was able to peel them myself. My oncologist said that if I could peel the fruit, I could eat it. That meant that grapes and berries were out of the question, but I was able to have oranges, bananas, mangoes, and apples.

After my transplant, I was careful with my use of raw vegetables. How I longed for a salad. I had to steam everything just to be sure I did not open myself up to having any complications. Raw foods may contain germs that could hinder your chance of recovery.

Make sure your juices and dairy products are pasteurized.

If you eat out, ask your server if you can have your food prepared fresh. I asked at Panda Express and they were happy to oblige.

I am a vegetarian so my choices are obviously different from that of someone who enjoys eating meat. Be sure the meat is cooked through properly and not red or pink in color.

Although I was limited in my choice of fruits and had to steam my vegetables, I consoled myself with the fact that it would only be for a short while before I would be able to resume my routine.

Friends

Although I had friends I could call on in the middle of the night and was able to do so when I found myself in difficulty, I don't recommend waking up your friends as a habit, but it's nice to know there is someone there you can call on when you need them. Usually though, something happens when one gets cancer. Sometimes friends have a hard time dealing with it, so you may go through a dry spell without seeing or hearing from anyone. They suddenly get very busy and have a lot going on in their lives. I believe this is all to avoid facing you and the situation. They may feel sorry for you and are not quite sure what to say or do. Some may even act as though nothing happened. It becomes awkward because the conversations are no longer the same. They may even question if they say the wrong thing, so avoidance is the result.

I believe God wants us to have friends to help lighten our load when we are weak and down, but if they disappear during the difficult time, would we really consider them friends anyway? We can be thankful then that we have a friend in Jesus who is always by our side. He said He would never leave us nor forsake us.

There is something to be said about having a good friend but they are few and far between. I have spoken with other cancer patients and find this to be true in many cases where their friends withdraw. Some folks are fortunate they have friends that stick by them through the thick and the thin.

Sometimes you may feel lonely, although you are not really alone. In my hospital, we had one hour of rounding when someone was always coming in my room every hour to do vitals or just to find out if I needed anything. My answer to the loneliness dilemma, when I was feeling up to it, I would start calling people. You can talk for quite a while to get over the feeling loneliness.

My RELAPSE:
A mere bump in the road

After leaving the hospital, I had frequent follow-ups with my hematologist who kept track of my disease. She did all the necessary blood work and checked to see how my disease was progressing. She recommended a particular drug to keep me in remission but I refused it. I was in remission and quite resistant to consolidation chemotherapy. I just couldn't understand why I would choose to make myself sick again after being sick for such a long time.

On Tuesday June 4th, 2013, I presented myself to my hematologist's office for a follow-up biopsy to keep track of my leukemia. She decided to do the bone marrow biopsy in her office, and to do this, meant she needed to give me medication to make me loopy so she could do the procedure with minimal amount of pain for me. She gave me a prescription for Percocet and Oxycodone, which I had to take the morning of the procedure before going to her office. It worked in that I was super-loopy, but it didn't work because I still felt the pain. I was so drugged; I was no good to myself. I walked into the office with help from my daughter and ended up leaving the office in a wheelchair. I spent the rest of the day so sick that a lined trash can became my close friend. I just don't handle drugs well. The truth is, I try to avoid drugs as much as possible. It is safe to say that I will never do that again.

A week after the biopsy, I suspected that something was not quite right, so I went to our Tuesday Morning prayer service and asked for prayers. I tried to be confident that whatever was about to come would only be a bump in the road that I had to travel on my journey with AML. I just knew there was a lot more to come before this journey would end.

On June 13, 2013, I went back to see my hematologist for the results of my bone marrow biopsy that had been done earlier. To my dismay she entered the room saying, "it's back." The leukemia had come back and it was now at forty percent meaning that forty percent of my bone marrow was now leukemia cells. Fear came over me. What now? After my startling discovery of a relapse, I was devastated to say the least. I felt a certain amount of guilt because I had chosen to try various types of natural remedies to keep my leukemia from coming back but was unsuccessful in keeping it at bay. It was back.

It was scary to be back in that position again, especially remembering what I had already experienced with getting to my first remission. Would I make it to remission again or would this be the end of the road for me? I chose then to believe that the God who brought me through to the first remission would do it again. Was I being presumptuous? God promised He would forgive my sins even presumptions, and heal all my diseases.

Psalm 145:13-19 says, "The Lord never breaks His promises; He is gracious in everything He does. The Lord helps those who are in trouble and lifts the load of those who are weak." I was in trouble and needed all the help I could get. Here we are again, where we had to make the decision for treatment to beat this horrid disease a second time. This time my hematologist chose a bone marrow transplant center (BMT) in Orlando. She thought they had a good team. She called the director of the program who told her to send me over. I trusted her judgment so I went home and prepared myself to spend another twenty-one days in the hospital.

I drove myself to the hospital because I thought my children who lived out of town might fly in and could use the car to get around. I took the scenic route so to speak, looking at the cows along the way. I took as long as I could; I was in no hurry to lock myself away for another three weeks. I also needed time to think. Why didn't I listen to my hematologist and take the Vidayza to keep this thing at bay? Why was I so stubborn about it? Did God have something in store for me? Jeremiah 29:11 says He has a plan for me. Did I thwart that plan by refusing the drug? Was I just naïve to think I could do something with the natural remedies to keep it away? I needed more time than I had to figure out all these questions. I went over several of them as I traveled to the hospital.

I made it to the hospital and parked the car in the garage close to the entrance so the kids could see it readily, but as it turned out, no one needed the car, so it sat in the parking garage for the entire time I was in the hospital. I had concerns about the car being towed because I thought it would look suspicious being in the same spot for such a long time. I was told that security would be alerted so there was no need to worry.

God Wanted Me Here

When I got to the hospital it was pretty late in the day, and since I took my time getting there, it was well after 5:00 p.m. when I arrived. Then I was told I could not be registered because I was out of network for my health insurance. That was a big deal for me, since any expenses incurred would be costly and could not be guaranteed to be paid by my insurance company.

I was at the point of tears. Here I was in a different city, all packed and nowhere to go. My head started pounding and everything that could go wrong did go wrong. I was now aching all over, eyes burning, fatigue — just an overall feeling of ill health possibly due to the knowledge that the leukemia was back.

The folks in the registration office were kind. The office manager offered to push me in a wheelchair to the emergency room so someone could take a look at me. I was still not sure if that meant "out of network" as well, so I called my insurance company and explained my situation and they told me what I needed to do. All together it was a long process before my insurance concern was settled and I was admitted.

The Journey Continues

*I*n the ER I was evaluated, then I was taken to the bone marrow transplant unit, where for some reason I felt relaxed, although I did not know what to expect. It was after 11:00 p.m. by the time I got to the floor. My first encounter was with a nurse who was helpful and reassuring as he took care of me. I now had no fear. I met with the doctors the next morning and it turned out that I had to start chemotherapy that night. I completed the treatment and I was released from the hospital on July 9th and advised to see my hematologist in Melbourne, FL on July 11. My cell counts were still not where they should be but were on the upward trend so they sent me home. I just wore a mask whenever I left the house.

My brother Philmore and his wife Valerie came from Atlanta and stayed with me at my home as I recuperated.

They drove me to appointments and prepared my meals. I tried to manage on my own but found I did not have the energy. I found it hard to ask for help. I still needed to learn that asking for help is not a sign of weakness. It's hard for me to ask for help. I am willing to do anything for others but it is hard for me to accept help from others. I hope I will learn this valuable lesson and that it will become easier as I go through this journey. By the time I saw my hematologist on July 11th, the cell counts had increased so that I could remove my mask. On July 18th, I went back to Orlando to have a bone marrow biopsy and was told then that I was indeed in remission again. Glory to God!

My joy was short-lived however, because my doctor wanted me to be back in the hospital on July 24th for consolidation chemotherapy. I had previously refused consolidation because I could not understand why I would be in remission and then go back for more chemotherapy. I was going again from a point of strength to a point of weakness and I was not happy to do that.

I went back to the hospital however, because I would do whatever was required in order for me to have the bone marrow transplant. I was expecting a mild form of the drug this time, but found it to be worse than the original treatment. The doctor had promised that if I could get to remission, he would consider doing the bone marrow transplant. It was therefore necessary for me to have the chemotherapy to stay clean for the transplant so I agreed. Three weeks later, here I was. I lost my hair again; it was just beginning to look nice. I could curl and style it and was beginning to enjoy the new short look, and just like that, it was gone.

During the periods, in the hospital waiting for my counts to come back, I sometimes needed blood products. My cell counts would fluctuate and one day it could have become so low that I would have to have a transfusion. It was never fun to hear at the beginning of the day that I would need blood products. I was always concerned about interaction even if I had Benadryl on board. On August 12, 2013, my cell counts started to come back and I was discharged again on August 15, 2013. The plan at that time was for me to return to the hospital on September 3 for more chemo and a stem cell transplant.

GOD'S IN CHARGE

I left the hospital fully expecting to return for admission in two weeks, but was later informed that the date has been changed to September 10th. The transplant coordinator called because they were concerned about the possibility of not having the stem cells at the time we would need it for the transplant. As the doctor told me, once he pulled the trigger he would not be able to undo it. The chemotherapy I would receive before the transplant was given to destroy my immune system and prepare for the donor cells. Not having the stem cells to infuse could mean certain death since I would no longer have an immune system. What a situation to be in. For safety's sake then, they felt it would be advisable to have the cells ahead of time. It would make them feel much more comfortable having the cells and freezing them until they were needed.

As a result, I got an extra week at home, which I desperately needed. The changing of the date for me was providential. I was having problems with my stomach caused by the previous round of chemotherapy and God knew it. I kept having the urge to throw up as well as severe stomach pains. One night previous to this occurrence, I had to call my friend Arlene. I did not want to call her again. It was pretty late at night when she came over and I felt awful about disturbing her after midnight. This night, even after I had done everything I knew to do, the pain became severe. I started throwing up and was a bit scared to be alone, so I called my neighbor Mae and asked her to come over. I felt awful because it was again past midnight, but I just didn't feel I should be alone. I was writhing with pain on the floor, to the sofa, then to the chair just trying to find a spot that I could feel comfortable enough to relax with hopes that the pain would subside. My neighbor suggested that we go to the ER but I said no. She started giving me warnings in increments of half an hour to see how I felt, before asking me again if I was ready to go the ER. I kept saying no. This went on for almost two hours. I was afraid to go to the ER because I did not know what they would do, and I knew it was only the chemo effect on my stomach. After all, I was only home because I was waiting for the date to go back to the hospital to have the stem cell transplant. I wanted nothing to interfere with that. I knew it was my stomach but I had no idea what to do about it. I decided that the next time she asked about going to the ER, I would give in. She asked me again, and I said "all right," but I dawdled a bit and took my time getting to the front door. We were going to go in her car parked in the driveway. When we opened the front door to leave, there sat a raccoon looking straight at us. I was fortunate enough to have a screen door between us. The animal did not move. It looked at us like a pet waiting for food. I hit the screen with my purse and it scampered off. At this time the ER visit didn't seem quite so important. We were now both afraid to go outside. We had no idea if the animal was still out there or if it had gone back to wherever it came from. We both decided we were not going out.

She thought the animal could have been rabid. She said she was uncomfortable with the fact that the animal was not afraid of people, and thought that it may be crouching under her vehicle parked in the driveway.

She decided to spend the night on the sofa and I slept in the chair. After trying several remedies, the pain finally subsided and I did not go to the ER.

It is entirely possible that this may have been a coincidence, but I truly believe that God did not want me to go to the ER that night and He found a way to stop us. There was really nothing to be done for me at the ER. I was able to see the doctor in Orlando the next day and I got the medication I needed to take care of the problem so I would be ready for my new scheduled transplant date.

The weekend of the August 31st was my birthday and I was all prepared to spend it alone and make the best of my situation. That Friday night — the day before my big day — I heard a knock at the door. It was almost bedtime so I was somewhat concerned about who would be visiting so late at night. It turned out to be my children coming from Maryland and Virginia to surprise me for my birthday. What excitement! Not only did they show up to surprise me, but they also brought my dog along to visit. I was ever so happy and thankful for their visit. I just love and appreciate them for their consideration. How happy I was to see my dog that I hadn't seen for over two months. He was living with my daughter in Maryland while I was in and out of the hospital. It was a wonderful surprise and the best gift I could have gotten. I really missed Austin and this was a special treat.

Saturday the 31st was my birthday and I attended church to give my testimony and ask for prayer for my upcoming procedure: the stem cell transplant. That night after taking my medication, I was feeling pretty good, so when my daughter asked what I wanted to do for my birthday, I said bowling. I had not bowled in years and felt good enough to try it. I bowled terribly; I was just too weak to keep the nine-pound ball rolling down the lane to get even one strike. I did pick up a spare which generated some excitement, but I could not break one hundred, this from a former league bowler. I refused to admit that my whole physical body had changed and I was no longer able to do what I used to.

Three days went by and then it happened. I was not able to use my right arm and I was in extreme pain. How silly of me? I was just beginning treatment for my stomach and now my arm. I felt I was in so much trouble, because I was supposed to be admitted for my bone marrow transplant in a week. I contemplated going to see my primary care physician, but decided against it because my stomach was in no condition to tolerate NSAIDS and I was sure that was going to be the prescription for an over-use injury. Then I thought he might even send me for X-rays to see what was actually going on before treating me. What was I thinking? I tried treating it myself with a heating pad, Icy Hot patches, and muscle strain cream, and ice packs/tylenol for the pain.

Before the week was over, the transplant coordinator called again to say they had pushed the procedure date back again another week. I said thank you Jesus. I was not ready to go in the hospital while having such difficulty with the use of my limb. I was having severe difficulty with moving my arm even to get dressed. I could not shift the gear in the car or even open the refrigerator door. I was in trouble with no one to help me. It was a nice outing for my birthday, and I had a really good time bowling, but that was quite a setback for me. The kids were now gone back home and I was in pain with a limited range of motion. God saw all of this. Even in our foolishness, He makes a way.

I don't know what God had planned but He certainly overrules in the affairs of men and I chose to believe that this again was all God's providence. I don't believe any of this was coincidence. I was a bit disappointed, but I also knew I needed the time to heal. I decided that this transplant would be done on God's timeline.

GOD DOES NOT MAKE MISTAKES

"*O*ur God is an all wise Father who knows the end from the beginning, who knows all the causes and all the outcomes, and who never makes a mistake" (*Desire of Ages*, pg. 224). God never leads His children other than where they would choose to be led if they could see the end from the beginning, and discern the glory of the purpose that they are fulfilling as co-workers with Him. *Help in Daily Living* (pg. 19) says, "As we commit our ways to Him, He will direct our steps."

After reading many articles on the subject, this view of God as an omniscient Father came into focus clearly for me as I went through my journey with leukemia. I knew God was in control and I knew that He could see the big picture. I knew He wanted the best for me and

I knew if I committed my way to Him that He would direct my steps, but somehow I had to be able to put all this together to make sense for my situation. So while I didn't know why the plans for my transplant did not work out, I could be assured that God had a plan and I just had to trust Him.

Through this whole ordeal I got more advice than I knew what to do with. They came from just about everyone I knew. For whatever reason they felt I needed to hear it, I heard it. I

had folks who tried to offer words of encouragement and others who just didn't think about the impact of their words. I truly believe these were well-meaning folks who felt that my situation would be much improved if I prayed a certain way. I needed to pray according to their way of thinking or specific beliefs. Some felt I needed to pray to God for exactly what I needed and He would do it. Some said that if I named it, I could claim it. Of course, I did not believe the same way. I felt that would be more like demanding something from God, and telling Him I wanted it done now. One woman even said, "Failure to receive the expected result was not an option." I was not sure what that meant, but it occurred to me that I would be telling God what to do for me instead of asking for God's will to be done in my situation. I even had one person insinuate that my condition would not improve until I receive what they were speaking into my life. How do you receive something if you don't believe it? This was quite a dilemma. I chose instead to lay my circumstances and my requests before the Lord and ask for an answer according to His will. Only He would decide who my donor would be and that would be that.

Sometimes we pray but what we want is not what God wants for us. His ways are not ours. He knows the outcome; do we dare tell Him how to work His plan? It is God's will that we pray especially in time of need, but I believe that we must leave the results with Him — our God who never makes a mistake. I know that He knew what I was going through, He knew my anxieties and my fears, and I only had to trust that the outcome would be His perfect will for me.

After one of my chemotherapy treatments, I had to have a bone marrow biopsy and as a result I had to have an IV line put in. The individual placing the line had difficulty getting into the vein. The only one she felt was viable was on the back of my hand. Trying to access that vein was painful for me. Not being someone with a high threshold for pain, I cried out asking God to help me. There was bleeding from the site that needed two washcloths to clean it up. After the ordeal, I reflected on what had just occurred. What exactly was I asking God to do? Stop the pain? Have her find another vein? I certainly wasn't equipped to determine what I needed to be done at that time. I only knew I needed relief from the pain. I had no idea what He would do but I asked for help and I was confident He was there and He would do something.

I knew the line was not placed well because the pain never subsided throughout the period of waiting to be taken in to have the procedure done. Usually when the line is placed well, the pain goes away, but it didn't in this case. There was constant pain and I was afraid to move my arm. I was finally taken into the procedure room where they administered the drug to put me to sleep – conscious sedation. After the procedure, I had to have blood drawn in another area of the hospital so they decided to use the line that was already placed. When they tried to flush the line, all the saline pooled under the skin leaving a big, dark (more like black and blue) circle on the back of my hand that was painful for days. The phrase they used was "you blew a vein." The veins on the back of the hand are small and she just had to hit it right. I could be wrong medically, but I felt that God helped me in holding things together so I could make it through the procedure without having to have another line placed — my worst fear.

In my suffering I wondered if suffering was part of God's will for me. "Wherefore let them that suffer according to the will of God commit the keeping of their souls to Him in well doing, as unto a faithful creator." (1 Peter 4:19) As Christians, we aren't promised that we will be free from suffering. We suffer for various reasons, but if we are committed to the God who never makes a mistake, we can have the assurance that He has permitted our suffering and has a specific reason for it. We don't know, but God just might be doing something special in making us what He wants us to be. I believe it's in the suffering and the hard times that we learn to say, "Lord I want only your will because you never make a mistake."

In Job 2:10, Job asked his wife the important question that faces us today: "Shall we accept good from God and not trouble?" Job accepted that both prosperity and affliction were coming from God so he was willing to submit to His will. In the middle of the pain, I was not able to endorse the feeling of Job, but I had to believe that as hard as it may be for me, I had to understand that whatever God sent to me was always that which was best for me and could in fact be a blessing in disguise.

In my finite mind I couldn't see it so I had to trust in faith. I would like nothing more than to be healed and restored, but I have to be willing to say, "Thy will be done," because I believe that God does not make mistakes.

THE WAITING ROOM *

$\mathcal{W}$e have all heard the old cliché that patience is a virtue. Is it really? The word *patience* is defined as "waiting without complaint," or, "calmly tolerating delay." In my case this definition was spot-on correct. I don't consider myself to be virtuous but I recognized that waiting on God's timing was paramount in my situation of life and death. I knew there was no need to complain because it would change nothing. Yes, sometimes I cried and felt sorry for myself but soon enough, I got over it.

Prior to this time, my donor and I were given a calendar with a schedule of events that should take place up to and including the day of the bone marrow transplant. Here we were and not one of the events on the calendar went as planned. As it turned out, my sister Audrey who was my stem cell donor had an infection from a tooth.

Her doctor gave her antibiotics to take care of it but somehow it was not resolved. She went to the hospital to complete all the preparations required before the day of the transplant and found that they could not begin her Neupogen shot because her white count was already too high. These shots are normally given for four consecutive days prior to harvesting the stem cells, so as to produce a greater population of cells. Because her white cell count was already high, the date of harvesting her cells was postponed.

We had hoped that she would be able to follow the schedule that was given. Unfortunately three weeks later, I was still waiting for a transplant date. That schedule slipped so many times, each time one week later. I had to trust that God was in control and knew what was best for me in that period of my life I was in that I called, "the waiting room." God is sovereign therefore He overrules in everything that concerns me. I found it difficult and even challenging to be patient when I tried to see things from my own perspective. *Waiting* for me meant *trusting* and that's hard. Proverbs 3:5 says, "Trust in the Lord with all thine heart and lean not on your own understanding." I had to return to basics – that is, the decision I made in Tampa during my second round of chemotherapy.

I agreed to give up my desire for control and surrender every aspect of my life to Christ. Whatever happened would be God's responsibility and no longer a weight on me. The load can get pretty heavy when I try to carry it on my own. Isaiah 40:31 says, "They that wait upon the Lord shall renew their strength." How simple it was to get relief. I just had to wait; yet I still had the desire to control and fix things. I couldn't fix this. It was out of my hands and I was completely dependent on my donor and God. I was reminded of Lamentations 3:25-26, "God is good to those who wait for Him, to the soul who seeks Him. It is good that one should hope and wait quietly for the salvation of the Lord." I also knew that the Bible says in Matthew 6:34, "Do not be anxious about tomorrow," and as hard as I tried, I couldn't keep the anxious thoughts away on my own. I still worried about what was going to happen next. I chose then to accept the difficulties I had as God working in me to build patience, something that was sadly lacking in my character.

During this period of waiting, someone shared a devotional with me about waiting. Gal. 6:9 says, "Don't be weary in well doing for in due season we shall reap if we faint not.".I questioned what being weary in well doing had to do with my situation now. Then I got the explanation that "due season" was the period when God decided the time was right not when we think it should be. God had a set time for what He wanted to accomplish in my life so all I had to do was settle down and wait because that's when it would happen and not one day or one minute before. I decided I would go along for the ride as I anxiously waited to see what the outcome would be. In spite of the ups and downs, God had a plan. In spite of the disappointments and sufferings I experienced, God was working all things out for my good (Romans 8:28). He is never absent and He is never late, He is always on time. So here I wait.

Journal entry:

I have been out of the hospital for a month now, and today I had to go for an appointment with the hematologist who informed me that if my donor was not cleared this week. I would have to be back in the hospital for another round of chemotherapy. This is necessary because, as he puts it, if the Leukemia comes back I might not make it back to remission again and I need to be in remission before they could do the transplant. It seemed that things were going from bad to worse. I could only pray, "Lord please help my donor to be healthy." I was not sure that my body could handle another round of chemo. I had already had four of them.

Days later, I received a call from the transplant coordinator who told me they could not use my donor as she was no longer a viable candidate, so we had to go back to square one.

That meant I would be required to go back to the hospital for another round of chemotherapy. I was totally discouraged. It seemed to me that I spent more time in the hospital than I did out of the hospital. I had been in the hospital in June, July, and August. It was now September and I should have been back to the hospital in September for a bone marrow transplant, but my donor fell through. Lord, how do I handle this? As I struggled to deal with my new reality, I was again reminded that God has a plan for me and it's not to harm me. As usual, whenever I was in trouble and I needed answers,

I would read. So I went to the Word to find something to take me through this one. I found that when Jesus promised He would never leave me, He meant in the hard times as well as the good times so all I had to do was watch and continue to wait to see what God was going to do next to accomplish His purpose.

Someone said, "Every disappointment is God's appointment." I knew He would do something but what? He promised "no good thing would He withhold from me," so while I waited, I cried and I prayed, and I cried.

I did not want to have another round of chemotherapy and this being out of the hospital for so long and my needing to be in remission for the transplant were two good reasons to do another round of chemotherapy.

The next day my oncologist called to say he was sorry about the way things turned out. He said that he spoke with my sister Valerie and she agreed to come to Florida in two weeks so they could work her up as a donor for me. He would therefore postpone the chemotherapy pending the transplant. Then he asked, "Does that make you happy?"

Only the Lord knew how happy I was. I just kept praising Him saying, "Thank you Jesus." I had been reading and I found encouragement from a book by Ruth Myers called *31 days of Praise*. As I read, I decided I would praise God before my results were evident. I praised Him as if it was already done. I praised God for being sovereign over the big things in my life as well as the little details. I admitted that with Him nothing was an accident or coincidence. I thanked God that with Him, no experience was wasted. As I journeyed through this crisis, I learned to trust Him even more. The Bible tells me that He holds in His power my breath of life and my destiny all I had to do was trust Him. Why do we find it so hard? I truly believed that every trial that He allowed to come to me was a means of revealing Himself to me. He was showing His love and power to me and to others who may be watching to see how I would handle this.

I thanked Him that I was able to trust Him in this situation; I thanked Him that I could move into the future to whatever was ahead because I really felt He was going to come through for me. I knew that He held my future in His hands and I was even more confident because He promised me in Hebrews that He would be with me even to my old age.

FACING DEATH

*A*s a young girl, I was required to memorize many poems as well as scripture passages. One such piece that came to mind during this time was the quote from Julius Caesar that says, "Cowards die many times before their deaths, the valiant never taste of death but once." Why I remembered this at this particular time I cannot explain except — of course — my fear of needles. I have to admit that to some extent, this was adequately describing me in this situation.

Every day as I waited for the days to pass before the date of the stem cell transplant, I would reflect on what was to come. Each time I would shudder at what I thought was ahead of me and even played it out in my mind how painful it was going to be. I guess you could say I died a little each time. I know what the Bible says about faith and trust in God, but somehow controlling my thoughts was quite a different story. I dreaded the day that I would have the trifusion catheter put in. I had questions like, how would I react to someone else's stem cells? Will my body accept or reject it? "Only time will tell" was my answer before snapping back to reality.

I fully intended and resolved to be valiant, but as time passed my resolve weakened and I was back to the stage of the coward. These were the times when I had to remind myself that God was in control and I had nothing to fear. I knew I was not afraid to die, but I was not willing to embrace it either. I finally accepted the fact that this disease could take me out, but I also had to trust that God had other plans. So in the face of death, I would fight to stay alive doing all that was required of me, putting one foot in front of the other even when I didn't feel like it. Even though I was constantly reminded of the brevity of life, I was determined to cooperate with God to stay alive. Although I was not always able to control my thoughts and needlessly struggled, I could choose to believe by faith that God is sovereign, that He was holding me in His loving hands so that I could face the uncertainties and dangers of the transplant with confidence. James 4:14 says, "You do not even know what will happen tomorrow," but God does. I was scared. Plain and simple.

I started reading the scriptures to encourage myself. Psalm 118:6: "The Lord is with me; I will not be afraid." 1 Peter 5:7: "Cast all your anxieties on Him for He cares for you." Last was the 23rd Psalm, one of the scripture passages I had to memorize as a child: "Yea though I walk through the valley of the shadow of death I will fear no evil: for Thou art with me thy rod and thy staff they comfort me."

I prayed for strength to be valiant in the face of this looming problem. I prayed for wisdom to deal with controlling my thoughts and for God to do something for me to calm my emotions and my anxieties. I thanked Him that He knew and wanted what was best for me and I thanked Him that no situation — not even this one — was beyond His control and that I was extremely grateful that I could trust Him with my life.

THE SIGNING

*B*efore having the transplant, the doctor had to have a session with me when he would tell me all that the law required him to disclose before I could sign the consent forms for the procedure. In order to be compliant, I believe, he was just brutally honest with what he had to say. To help me remain positive, I decided that it was just the worst case scenario and that it really didn't apply to me. He told me that for those having a bone marrow transplant there is usually only a forty percent survival rate. That was all I heard. Would I be one of the sixty percent? I wondered. I was so trans-fixed on that forty percent that I didn't hear much else. Yes, he was talking but I didn't hear what he said. I thought about my second round of chemotherapy in Tampa when the doctor gave me fifty percent. I thought that was bad, and it weighed quite heavily on me then, but I remembered my neighbor saying, "whose report will you believe?" Strangely enough, hearing the low odds this time did not have the same effect as it did before. I couldn't explain it, except to say I chose to believe that God who brought me through the fifty percent was going to defy the odds again because He has the last word. Whatever the outcome, I had two choices: trust God and go ahead or not do the transplant. There was no middle ground. I had to see this through to the end, so I prayed that I would be one of the four people who would survive, I placed the whole decision in God's hand and moved on. The anxiety dissipated as the peace of God flowed in. There was no way to explain that. It just happened. I asked the nurse to have the doctor come back and explain the rest to me because I missed everything he said after the forty percent. He came back and tried again to explain, this time softening the blow a bit. I still don't remember what he said but I signed the pages and initialed where it was needed. I had settled it in my mind that God was able and I had nothing to worry about.

Earlier that day for devotion I read a chapter from a book by Mark Finley. In his sermon "The Best is Yet to

Come", I was encouraged that whatever was going to happen would be what was best for me and that it would be according to God's will. Leaving home that morning, I fully expected that I would be distressed driving back home from Orlando. I thought that I should have had someone accompany me for the bad news, but after signing the consent form, I was at peace knowing that God was in charge.

THE TRANSPLANT

By definition, a bone marrow transplant (also referred to as a stem cell transplant) is a procedure that transplants healthy bone marrow (stem cells) into a patient whose bone marrow is not working. The fact that I had a relapse would suggest to me that my bone marrow was not working. As I understand it, once the bone marrow is infused, the stem cells migrate to the bones and the cells begin to divide. If everything goes well, my bone marrow is entirely replaced by the cells of my donor. The procedure however, is not without risk, because once my white cells are destroyed by chemotherapy, it takes a while for the transplanted bone marrow to engraft and to produce new white blood cells to protect me against infection. The list of symptoms is quite long and could include: chest pain, headache, hives, nausea, chills, and a drop in blood pressure.

I was required to wear a mask every time I left the house or just to go outdoors. I knew there was always a risk of serious infection and I also knew there was a risk of rejection. There was also the possibility that the new bone marrow could produce active cells that could attack my body and cause what is called "graft versus host disease." We had to be careful to avoid complications that could include anemia, bleeding in the lung, brain, and other areas of the body. I started having headaches about one month after my transplant and had to have an MRI of my brain. Fortunately for me, there was no evident damage. There was also the risk of damage to the kidneys, liver and heart. The worst part of this whole process for me was the fact that in spite of a bone marrow transplant and my hope of recovery, the cancer may still recur. Understanding the process and all that could happen made me more determined that I had to turn the whole process over to God.

When I was presented with the possibility of having a bone marrow transplant, three of my siblings agreed to be tested to see if they were a match to be my bone marrow donor. My sister Valerie was first to be tested and it was determined that she was a positive match. My sister Audrey was also a match, but my brother Hugh was not. How wonderful, I had choices. When I stop to think that statistics says only about thirty percent of all potential stem cell transplant patients have family members whose antigen type matches their own, and here I was with two, I felt quite fortunate and very thankful to God for His provision.

My transplant team decided to use stem cells from Audrey possibly because she lived close to the hospital in St. Cloud outside of Kissimmee, Florida. While I was pleased to have two positive matches, I was still concerned because I was not sure what it would mean for them. When my first donor fell through, my team reached out to my other sister Valerie who lived in upstate New York, quite a distance from Orlando. The expense that would be involved was of concern to me and the time away from her family was also a concern. However, she agreed to go through the process and ultimately made her way to Florida within two weeks. It was important for me that she got to Florida as soon as possible, since a considerable amount of time had elapsed since my last chemotherapy treatment while I waited for my sister Audrey to be medically cleared. I did not want to have another round of chemotherapy before being admitted for my transplant. It would mean at least another twenty days in the hospital, not to mention the effect it would have on my body that had already been through a lot. My doctor was also concerned about my remaining in remission so he could do the transplant. It was a stressful time for me. I was sitting on pins and needles as I awaited my sister's arrival. I felt helpless. There was nothing I could do to expedite the process. I praised God she agreed to come and hoped that I would remain in remission for at least another two weeks. I prayed a lot and read a lot. I just had to trust that God would work it out all in His own good time. I wondered about my donor and whether she was sure of what she was getting herself into. Was this more than she bargained for? What will happen to her as a result? When I looked at the machine used to extract the cells and her lying there for hours, I wished she didn't have to go through that.

My cells were collected through a non-surgical process called "apheresis" in which blood is removed from the donor and the stem cells are extracted from the blood and the remaining components are returned to the donor. The cells they harvested were processed in the laboratory and infused into my body the same day through a trifusion catheter. The catheter was placed on me during the first day of admission to the hospital. It was placed in the area of the neck towards the heart and brought out on the chest area seven days prior to the procedure. It was similar to a blood transfusion.

They also placed a catheter for my donor since they needed a large vein for the procedure of harvesting the cells. Having the catheter placed must have struck some fear of what was to come for her. I was concerned about any pain she would feel as a result but I found out later that she has a high threshold for pain so it was not a problem for her.

I had so many questions and concerns that my emotions ran the gamut, more like a rollercoaster. I truly felt that if God was not with me I would have had a nervous breakdown, I was that close. I felt as though my knees would buckle at any given moment and I would fall to the floor in a heap, but He gave me strength for that crisis and others that occurred up to the point of actually getting the transplant. Once I made it through that and I was still standing, my next concern was whether or not I would survive the transplant. I had heard so many stories my brain could not process all the possible outcomes. It was only God who brought me through that intense period of mental calisthenics. I was encouraged, however, when my hematologist looked at me and as if he could tell what was going on inside, said, "I know you have connections, get in touch with it. You'll be all right."

I can't say enough about Dr. Khaled and his bone marrow transplant team. I had exceptional care and truly believe that they are a top-notch group of people whose only goal and desire is to see you get well. So what do you say to someone who saved your life? No words can do it justice. All I can say is I am eternally grateful for the gift I have been given.

As the days went by and I felt my new life coming back, I frequently thought about Valerie and her willingness to consent to go through the process despite the expense of flying to Florida and her hotel stay. To top it off, her husband flew down as well to be with her as she went through the process. It is not an ordinary thing, giving of oneself to help someone else. There are many who wouldn't consider it.

I know and have spoken with folks who were scared and reluctant to do anything of the sort especially if they thought it would cause them pain. They were just not willing to go through the process. I felt quite fortunate to get this gift, and especially so since my sister had recently retired. Had she been still working, as a schoolteacher, she would be in the classroom, which would have made it so much more difficult for her to get away. God had it all planned. I can clearly see now that God was in charge of this, long before I needed Him to work it out for me. I thank Him for the way He brought it all together in His time. Words are inadequate to convey my appreciation for the gift I have been given. I owe a lot to God for giving me life and my sister Valerie for saving that life. My plan is to finish strong, and to use my new found life to serve God with every fiber of my being.

For an entire week before the transplant, I was given a potent combination of chemotherapy drugs, with the aim of not only destroying the cancer cells in my body but also to erase any healthy bone marrow that remained. Prior to the infusion I was given a painkiller and an antihistamine to reduce the severity of infusion reactions if it should occur.

During the transplant, my transplant team had a nurse seated next to my bed for as many hours as it took to complete the infusion process. Her job was to monitor my vital signs and look for the slightest sign of irregularities and hoping that my body would accept the new life I was being given. I saw her sitting there while I went in and out of consciousness. I didn't know why she was there but I was told later and was glad to know someone was close by just in case. She was so close she could hear my feint whisper. While she was sitting there, I believe that angels were hovering over my bed to make sure there would be no irregularities for her to report. When I awoke the transplant was over and the nurse was gone, though I have no idea who she was or what she looked like, I believe Jesus was there with me. October 14th was day zero of my new birth; the day my new physical life began.

Twenty-one days later when my doctor came in for his usual rounds, he was smiling and somewhat elated. He said I was doing so well he was considering sending me home in two days.

After answering a few of my many questions he began to leave the room. I don't know what came over me, maybe the excitement of knowing I was doing well or the excitement at the prospect of going home. I don't know, I just shouted out, "Wait! Shouldn't we have a prayer or something? This is great news!"

He asked, "do you want *me* to pray?"

I said, "Yes!"

Not wanting to delay his rounds I assume, he said okay then he looked up to the ceiling and said, "I didn't do this. You know I didn't do this, but thank you for helping me to help Arline and anyone else that will come through these doors."

He began to move toward the door as I said, "Amen." One of the doctors with him whispered to him, "you are supposed to say amen when you are done." He said he didn't know and they all left my room smiling about the event that had occurred. I was amazed at what had just taken place and was overjoyed that my non-Christian Egyptian doctor prayed. I could not believe that he prayed and though he never said "God", I was satisfied. I felt that God reached out to him that day and I believe He will go to any length to reach His children. Who knows if my illness was not a means of reaching him? I'd like to think so.

MY RECOVERY

The recovery period — the days and months that followed the transplant — were challenging ones and a time of great risk and concern. There was always a high risk for infection during the first few weeks while I was still in the hospital and even after leaving the hospital. Leaving the safety of the hospital was scary. After leaving the hospital I was extremely weak and tired all of the time. In addition, I sometimes felt unsteady on my feet. There was the fear of rejection, the weakness, nausea, and fear of infection all put together, receiving someone else's cell into my body sometimes seemed unbearable and caused me to question my decision. I agreed that I would fight this disease; I agreed that I would go down fighting. It would not be because I did not try, but the waiting to return to normal after the procedure was quite a challenge that took some strength to overcome.

I knew my body needed time for Valerie's blood cells to engraft and I needed to be patient so I prayed. I prayed for patience as I went through every blood test and bag of IV drip, as I waited to see the results, as I waited for my strength to return, as I waited for the nausea to subside — I prayed. Waiting is hard... I had to go to the clinic three times per week then my visits became less as I progressed. Thank God for His faithfulness to me.

While I waited, I had to learn how to cope. It had been two years of treatments, remission and relapse and now living away from home. I wanted nothing more than for this to end. There was so much to avoid in order for me to stay healthy during my recovery that sometimes I wondered if I did the right thing or even if I had the strength to go through it all.

My team was ever so vigilant to make sure I did not get an infection. They were constantly checking to be sure I had no mouth sores, diarrhea, or rashes. I had my brother Philmore and his wife as my caregivers for the first month after my transplant. Their service was invaluable. I could not have managed without them. It just took so much out of me; it was good to have someone I could count on to share how I was feeling and to give me advice as to how to handle each situation when they occurred. For some reason it was difficult for me to make some decisions which in the past would have been a no-brainer for me. What happened? I didn't know and I found it hard to explain.

I was concerned about them leaving because it meant that after they left, I would have to play a more important role in my own health care which included fixing meals, taking my medications as directed, as well as driving myself to each appointment at the cancer center to meet with the transplant team. It was not easy and I did not feel ready to go it alone, I was just not up to the challenge. The worst was the driving. Usually, after negotiating the traffic on the busy highway, I would get to the parking lot at the hospital and sit for a few minutes to compose myself before trying to go inside. I felt tired and was still weak and nervous. I was afraid that I would overreact or overcorrect in the fast moving traffic pattern. My legs would shake in the middle of a large intersection and I was constantly afraid of being hit.

Each time I had to go to the clinic I hoped that I would make it safely without incident. I prayed constantly that God would take charge of my vehicle. I had so many almost-accidents that I know God had to be there with me. As the weeks went by, I got better at it. When my doctors changed the frequency of my visits, I returned to my home in Palm Bay. It was farther away from the hospital, but a less stressful drive to get there.

I was happy to be out of the hospital and enjoyed the freedom of going outdoors. I remembered the days when I sat by the huge glass windows wishing to be outdoors and wondered when it would happen. I knew I should be grateful because there were others that did not make it home and others that made it home and had to return. For the first thirty days after leaving the hospital, I did well and I constantly prayed that there would be no complications as I progressed through the recovery period.

I knew there were many risks in receiving someone else's cells as the new bone marrow can cause any number of problems all labeled as "graft versus host disease" or GvHD. The new bone marrow (the graft) is the new immune system which can reject the body it is transplanted into (the host) and can potentially attack any part of the body. The first time I heard I might have GvHD, I panicked because I felt this was not good and I had no idea what I could do to prevent it. My fears were allayed when I later found that GvHD was not all life-threatening, but that the disease could range from mild to life-threatening and may occur anytime within my first one hundred days.

After my transplant I had some skin discoloration issues that were described as GvHD, but not really an issue of concern. Thankfully I was not experiencing any further complications except for the skin discoloration. I was so concerned about this issue that I tried to closely follow the guidelines given to me so as to reduce the risk of life-threatening infections and other complications. Because of this fear, my doctor wanted me to stay close to the hospital so my commute to get there would be less than an hour. I stayed with my sister Audrey in St. Cloud outside of Orlando. I was thankful to her for opening her home to me for such an extended period of time.

It had been a month since my discharge from the hospital and my children wanted us to spend Thanksgiving together at my home in Palm Bay. Secretly I believe they were uncertain of the outcome and not sure if we would ever meet again in that fashion, so they decided to come home. It was a pleasure for me to be able to see them again. Best of all for me, was that I could see my dog Austin again. However in order for this to happen, I had to consult with the doctors. To walk this fine line to recovery I had to adhere to all the rules and yes, I would if it meant I would get to see Austin.

My nurse Sean was so specific in his instructions that there was no misunderstanding what he said. The first thing was I could have dinner but mine had to be served first. If I felt I might need seconds, take it out at the same time. I could not go back after everyone had eaten. That was clear enough. The next thing was the dog. Austin is a white and beige mini poodle, still living in Maryland with my daughter Tricia. Some say poodles are smart dogs. I say mine was intuitive. My instruction for his visit was that I could visit with Austin but he could not lick me, an almost impossible feat since that's how dogs show their love. Also, I could not clean up after him. That was no problem since I had more than enough help for the holidays. The licking part was hard. I had to be stern with him in saying, "No lick," and somehow it seemed he understood. He just sat next to me on my big chair and placed his head on my lap.

God had been good to me. I had not experienced many complications and for that I was grateful. Thank God!

I was required to take an excessive amount of medications. I guess that was because of all the bacteria, viruses, and fungi that are all around us. I was given antifungal, antiviral, and antirejection drugs all to keep me healthy through recovery. Hugging and handshaking was definitely not the way to go, so when I did, I used a lot of hand sanitizers. I took all the drugs that were prescribed, and simply hoped for the best. My mornings were usually so beautiful until I took the medication, then I had the nausea and just a low feeling. I hated taking the meds because of the way I felt after taking them, but I knew it was for my own good so I took them. After a few minutes I would usually feel better and could continue with my day. I would sometimes say, "Where you are bound you must obey." I have no idea where that came from or who wrote it, but it's what I say when I have to do something I hate to do.

The side effects were tremendous. The nausea was relentless. I was so weak and tired and felt so sick it seemed there was no break in sight. I thankfully got medication that slowly improved my condition. I attended the clinic three times per week to start, and then twice per week so my doctors could keep a close eye on what was taking place with me during this recovery period. The frequency of my visit to the clinic lessened as time passed and I steadily improved.

Trying to eat healthy was a challenge as I found I had acquired drug-induced diabetes. I had a glucose level of 408, which took me by surprise. I had to limit my meals to consuming foods without sugar. Since then the doctors have been able to adjust the medication so that I now have an acceptable glucose level upon rising each morning.

One of the worst side effects was the awful metallic taste, so I tried to find the foods that had some sort of taste to me. I liked the foods that had a salty taste, which seemed to help with that metallic taste, but then I had to be careful about elevating my blood pressure. I basically found myself between a rock and a hard place, but with God's help I was able to get through each day.

I was determined to do whatever was required to help reduce infection risk and regain my strength.

I was told that if and when I got to one hundred days, my chances of survival would be substantially increased. I counted down the days and each week after my labs I would ask, "what day is this?" This wasn't really accurate or scientific because there were folks who were up to 90 days and had to be put back in the hospital. I guess it helped the psyche somewhat to have a marker of some sort by which one could measure their progress.

After completing my one hundred days post-transplant, I had what was hopefully my last bone marrow biopsy. I was confident that God would complete what He had started so after having the biopsy, I pushed it out of my mind and never thought about it again. I felt everything was going to be all right, because God was in control so I just didn't think about it again until I had to go back for the good news. The results revealed that my bone marrow was now ninety-nine percent my donor's, meaning the level of engraftment of the stem cells in my bone marrow from my donor was ninety-nine percent of my total bone marrow, which was simply awesome news. Additionally, there was no evidence of any leukemia cells present in my body! Dare I say the word remission? I am extremely grateful for the positive results. Praise God from whom all blessings flow.

I was then allowed to go to church and also have my dog back both with some restrictions. Then came the day I decided to attend church. I had not been to church in almost eight months, and now here I was driving with the Florida sunshine beating on my face. I called my sister Valerie to tell her because I knew she would have been excited to know I was strong enough to be on my way to church. Who would have thought that eight months ago? I was so excited I hardly slept the Friday night before. I tossed and turned and watched the clock. On Sabbath morning, I made my way to the church armed with my mask. When Pastor Phipps announced my return and welcomed me back, there were sounds of "Amen" coming from all corners of the sanctuary.

God had done it again and I was pleased that God's name was once again glorified. Altogether my first day back to church was a good day.

Murphy's Law

All through my life whenever something went wrong I would always say, "that's the story of my life; nothing good ever happens for me," and I would expect Murphy's Law to kick in. In most situations it did. That's just the way it worked for me. I truly regret the choices I may have made in the past that would have allowed this to be true in my life, but Praise God. Because of my relationship with Him through this illness and certainly after the final bone marrow biopsy report, I can never say that again. God in His mercy has seen it fit to save me. He took me from sickness to wholeness and from literally death to life. With every day that goes by, the expected length of my survival increases and I thank God for each day He allows me to be here. I understand that full recovery could take years before I can say I am cured but I'm well on my way.

I was reading the Leukemia & Lymphoma Society magazine that showed up unannounced at my home ever since I was diagnosed and a statement caught my attention. It said, "AML is a devastating blood cancer with less than twenty-five percent of newly diagnosed patients surviving beyond five years." Well now, this is the time for me to ask whose report I will believe? I have to believe that God did not bring me this far to leave me and that what He has begun He will be faithful to complete. So I go on in faith believing that the same God who defied the odds of fifty percent in Tampa and brought me to remission, and the forty percent survival after my transplant will also defy this twenty-five percent past five years. I don't believe God wants me to be constantly looking over my shoulder or waiting for the other shoe to drop. I settled it in my mind a long time ago, that God was able and I had nothing to worry about, because I know what He has done for me in the past and He will continue to perform it, Murphy's Law or not.

I continue to encourage myself with the text in 1 Peter 5:10 (NIV) which says, "And the God of all grace, who called you to His eternal glory in Christ, after you have suffered for a little while, will Himself restore you and make you strong, firm and steadfast."

My life no longer depended on Murphy's Law but on Jesus Christ who holds the keys of death and hell. He broke the cycle and allowed me to see that He was with me throughout my journey with this disease. Ultimately, whether I lived or died it would still have been the prerogative of God.

According to the opinion of some, at my age I was not supposed to have a stem cell transplant, but I did. Making it through recovery without complications is not normal, but it happened. I shouldn't have been driving at thirty days post-transplant, but I was, and only because God was with me every step of the way whether I felt Him near or not. Then there were those who expected I would die shortly after the diagnosis, but in God's wisdom, I'm still here. So now, when I say, "that's the story of my life," it won't be because something bad happened, but because I now have a new story. God has made good out of a bad situation. He has proven to me that I am a child of the King, a King who is truly concerned about every detail of my life; the

King who loves me with an everlasting love and is in charge of every situation that occurs in my life.

The song "Your Grace Still Amazes Me" written by Connie Harrington and Shawn Craig so aptly describe what God has been to me through my illness with blood cancer. It became even more evident when I received an invitation to the cancer survivors reunion celebration. All I can say is: "God, it's only through your Grace."

Your Grace Still Amazes Me

My Faithful Father, enduring friend, your tender mercy's like a river with no end It overwhelms me, covers my sin, each time I come into your presence, I stand in wonder once again.

Your Grace, still amazes me, your love's still a mystery, each day I fall on my knee, cause your grace still amazes me, your grace still amazes me

O patient Savior you make me whole, you are the author and the healer of my soul, what can I give you, Lord, what can I say, I know there's no way to repay you, only to offer you my praise

Thank you God: He never makes a mistake. He chose to give me back my life for a purpose. My goal now is to find that purpose. I am still completely dependent on God as to how this will all turn out. So rejoice with me as I seek to find His purpose and fulfill it. I hope this book has been a blessing for you and that you will experience God in your own way through whatever struggle you or your loved one may be facing right now.

EPILOGUE

My Cancer Diagnosis and its Spiritual Applications

*W*hen we hear that someone has cancer, it doesn't really mean much to us. Basically, we feel sorry for them because our first thought is that the person is going to die. Some of us will take the time to look on the internet to see what it's all about, and to check on the prognosis, but for the most part, it's not really a big concern until it hits home then we begin to think. What is the cancer going to do? How will it affect the life of the person with cancer? How will it affect their family? I've even been asked if it's contagious and whether they can still hug me. There are so many questions that demand an answer. I hope you were able to find at least some of your answers here.

The cancer that afflicted me was a blood cancer quite different from organ cancers that may require surgery and or radiation and chemotherapy. There is really nothing to cut out but a lot to destroy with the hope that when it's over I could still get up and walk away. Early in the beginning, I was told that without treatment I would die within three weeks. What a declaration. God however, had other plans.

I have long passed the time of asking "why" or "how come". God has taken me through the "valley of the shadow" and I just want to praise Him for where I am today. I prayed to God that all He has brought me through will be used as a means of encouraging others and that His name will be glorified through me as a result.

I also promised God that I would be a witness for Him through this trial and after reading Psalm 73:21-28, I was more determined than ever to do just that. As David said, I will tell everyone what God has done for me. It has been the desire of my heart for many years, to spread the gospel about the love of Christ. Whether it was through singing, health ministry, prison ministry, or literature evangelist work (selling religious books), it has all been in an effort to share the story of Jesus with someone who might be searching. I want to keep the promise that I made to almighty God so here I go.

My story is part of a bigger story, which is that God loves us and has a plan for our lives. That plan is to save us and to take us home to live with Him for eternity. The choice is and always has been ours, to accept Christ and His plan or go at it on our own. For years I have tried to do things on my own, seeking my own way until I met Jesus at a difficult time in my life and things began to change. I can now say I am thankful for the difficulties that prepared me for this journey with cancer. It could have caused me to lose my faith so many times. Through the struggles, it would have been so easy to give up, but because of the love, mercy, and faithfulness of God I am still standing after all is said and done.

I will never forget the day the oncologist/hematologist told me I had cancer. I will also never forget the day or the time when she told me it was back, after I had been in remission for only seven months. She said that there was no cure for this disease. Although there was no cure, there was something they could try called a bone marrow transplant that would possibly buy me more time. The problem with my body was, as I understood it, my white blood cells were multiplying faster than normal and making one bad cell after another. My bone marrow was packed with bad cells so that the good cells were literally choked out. My body was producing cells that were faulty. What the doctors needed to do then, was to destroy the whole system and hopefully find someone whose DNA matched mine closely enough grow a brand new immune system — a brand new blood system, if you will — from scratch.

They had to substitute someone else's perfect blood so I could have a new life, so I could live and not die. If I wanted to live I had to accept the offer to go through the process essentially accepting this gift of life from a donor. It was totally up to me; the choice was mine.

We have a sin problem that we cannot cure. The Bible says, "all have sinned and come short of the glory of God"; there is none righteous, no not one. We keep deceiving ourselves that we are okay. We are good people with good morals, but the Bible tells us that we are all sinners in need of a savior. When Adam and Eve sinned by their disobedience, they broke the face-to-face relationship they had with God so they hid from Him, their best friend. Sin had separated them from

God, and as a result sin was pronounced on all mankind. 1 Corinthians 15:22 says, "As a result of Adam's sin, all of us die. But because of Christ, all who believe in Him shall be made alive."

To solve the sin problem, God sent His son (your donor) to become the perfect substitute for us. God demonstrated His love toward us, in that while we were still sinners, Christ died for us. He had to die so that we might have eternal life. (Without the shedding of blood there is no remission of sin.)

All my doctors could offer me after going through the process was a few more years of remission instead of the seven months I had before at my first remission. God offers us eternal life. I was dying because of cancer and was in need of a transplant without which I would certainly die in a short time. I found a donor in the person of my sister who was willing to give her lifeblood so I could hopefully live a few more years. We are dying in our sins and are in need of a willing donor. We all have a donor in Jesus Christ who willingly paid the price and guarantees us eternal life.

My treatment began with a potent combination of chemotherapy drugs, the goal of which was not only to destroy the cancer in my body, but literally to destroy my bone marrow so I could receive the cells of my perfect match and as a result receive a new identity. A new birth, if you will. It was a slow death, so to speak and everyone involved waited to see if my body would receive the new life I had just been given. I was like a newborn baby again with a new birthday. I now had a new immune system with DNA that was not my own. If one should look at my blood today they will see my donor not me. It's no longer I who lives.

The same happens when we accept Christ as our substitute; He had to die a slow painful death on our behalf so we can have a new life. There is no price to pay; He already paid the price with the torture He experienced on the cross and the stripes on his body. John 3:16 states, "For God so loved the world that He gave His only begotten Son that whosoever believe in Him should not perish but have everlasting life." All we have to do is accept Him as our savior. It doesn't seem like a fair exchange, but that's the plan God put in place to save His children. He promises that He will come in to live in us then it will be no longer us but Christ living in us. All we need to do is receive Him through faith.

If there is any doubt in your mind while reading this, I encourage you to accept this free gift and pursue a relationship with Jesus Christ. You may obtain a beautiful relationship with Him today.

Understanding that our days on this earth are like a shadow, wouldn't it make sense to accept this perfect gift now? Tomorrow is not promised to anyone. David in Psalm 39 says our life is but a "hand's breath." Place your faith in Jesus as your savior and simply pray with a sincere heart something like the following prayer.

Lord Jesus, I open my heart to you. I confess that I am a sinner standing in need of your forgiveness. I know that I have sinned against you, and that my sins separate me from you, a Holy God. I am truly sorry, I repent now and want to turn away from my sinful past, and turn to you for forgiveness. Please forgive me. I believe that you died on a cross for me and that your blood was shed to blot out my sins. I invite you Jesus to become my Savior and the Lord of my life, to live in my heart from this day forward. Change my sinful desires and make me your child. Please send your Holy Spirit to help me obey you and to convict me when I go astray. I pledge to grow in grace and knowledge of you through daily reading your word. My greatest desire now is to follow your example and do your will for the rest of my life. In the name of Jesus I pray, Amen.

I included this in the book to help you understand that this journey of mine took a relationship with Jesus Christ, whom I want to offer to all who desire to know Him and have an intimate relationship with Him. The choice is yours. Choose Life. Blessings!

About the Author

Arline Farquharson

*A*rline was born in Jamaica West Indies, on August 31, 1945 and married in 1969. She worked for the Eastman Kodak Company as a Clinical Chemistry Laboratory Analyst for twenty-five years. She is now retired and living in Palm Bay, Florida where she worked as a Medical Coder for ten years until her retirement.

She has three grown children and four grandchildren. She enjoys singing and recorded her first project in 2000. She wrote articles for a Women's Devotional and for a hospital newspaper. She also compiled a Raw Food Recipe Book. Arline enjoys walking, painting, and gardening.

APPENDIX

Invitation

Save the Date
For the Florida Hospital Bone Marrow Transplant Reunion

Enjoy the afternoon of celebration and tribute at the Florida Hospital Bone Marrow Transplant Survivor Reunion. Entertainment and lunch will be provided.

Saturday August 9, 2014
12:00 to 4:00 pm

Double Tree by Hilton Orlando Downtown
60 South Ivanhoe Boulevard
Orlando, FL 32804

Attire is casual and seating is limited

This is the thank you card I sent after the final biopsy report

REJOICE WITH ME!
MY TRANSPLANT WAS
SUCCESSFUL!
Praise God!

Thank You for Your Prayers

CPSIA information can be obtained at www.ICGtesting.com
Printed in the USA
LVOW13s0224220814

400302LV00003B/3/P